# THE DOUGHERTY CODE

## SECRETS OF FINANCIAL PLANNING IN SPAIN REVEALED

PETER DOUGHERTY

The Dougherty Code
Secrets of Financial Planning in Spain Revealed

Copyright © 2023 by Peter Dougherty



ISBN: 979-8-9886232-0-5

Published by Dougherty Market Expansion LLC

Library of Congress Control Number: 2023912273

**THE PURPOSE OF THIS** book is to share my experiences as an American financial planner in Spain.

But my story doesn't begin there. No. I arrived in Spain already knowing enough Spanish to survive a job interview thanks to lots of language classes over the years. And lots of hard work. And more language classes. I studied Spanish in both South America and Spain, joined a Spanish book club in the States, and spent three years helping a not-for-profit group with orphanages in Central America.

You may have encountered people with a gift for languages. I'm not one of them. I've heard that for most of us, we need to allow a foreign language to drip—like drops of water into a sink, making sure there's a drain stopper in place—slowly over time into our consciousness. Turning on the faucet full blast does little good. Drip by drip, that's how I learned Spanish.

That's why I roll my eyes when I see ads like this: **"Learn a foreign language in 3 weeks!"**

So, I include "a few stories" of my language experiences at the end of this book to remind us that learning a foreign language can be fun, but it also requires more than 3 weeks of effort.

# CONTENTS

# INTRODUCTION

**T WAS IN 2018** that the seeds of this journey were first planted. It happened in Valencia, Spain. I was attending a language immersion school there and I made a habit of wandering through a certain leafy neighborhood. Keep in mind that the neighborhood was *never* on my way. Nonetheless, I made sure to pass through it every afternoon. While searching for a restroom there one day, I noticed the plaque of a private bank on the door of a building. Later, I saw a sign identifying yet a different bank.

"Oh, this neighborhood is Valencia's financial district!" I proclaimed loudly, though no one was around to hear me, "that's why I like it!"

I momentarily forgot all about needing to find the restroom.

This area was somehow reminiscent of the financial district of lower Manhattan to me. But smaller, with buildings that don't stand as tall. I'd spent years toiling away on Wall Street in lower Manhattan, in the financial hub of New York City.

"Wall Street" has now become more of a concept than an actual place; I'm told you can work on Wall Street without ever setting foot in New York. In my case, though, I'd worked for years near the New York Stock Exchange and the actual street named "Wall".

So, what had attracted me to this leafy financial district in Valencia, Spain—a stone's throw from Valencia's stock market – was that it reminded me of my financial career in New York. It brought back good memories. "How can I work in a financial environment like this *in Spain*?", I thought to myself.

———

It had been five years since I'd said goodbye to the financial district in New York. Why did I leave? Not long before that, a neighbor of mine had asked me: *"I've got this IRA bond fund. I need to make a required minimum withdraw this year; I started collecting Social Security a year after I'd qualified so it's 8% higher than I would've otherwise received. When and how much should I withdraw?"*

I didn't know. I'd worked as a bond specialist at investment banks for twenty years. Even today only a handful of people in the U.S. know what I do regarding a certain type of bond. But that wasn't going to help him.

And that really bothered me. You may notice that there's no GLOSSARY OF TERMS in this book. If I can't explain a concept in an understandable way, why am I discussing it at all? I take some pride (perhaps unjustified) in being able to remove the "financial jargon" from explanations if it enhances our ability to understand a financial theory or two.

I thought about it. To my neighbor, why wouldn't someone who worked with bonds every day be able to explain his bonds to him and help him make decisions about them? Looking at it from his perspective made perfect sense.

When I began my career, I never expected the knowledge and experience I gained on Wall Street to be of practical use in the everyday world. But it was interesting work, and I became good at it. Over time I focused on an increasingly narrow subsection within the wider world of bonds: assisting corporations in issuing bonds paying interest which, in most cases, is exempt from U.S. Federal income taxation to the buyers of the bonds.

And *that* is what bothered me about my neighbor's question. It caused me to ask myself *why* I worked in an area of finance so specialized that I couldn't offer advice on everyday questions about bonds? An area so particular, in fact, that I could offer expert advice only to knowledgeable corporate treasury teams who already had such bonds on their books or who wanted to issue them, but not to my neighbor if he had a basic question.

Is it surprising that I turned in my resignation at Bank of America Merrill Lynch soon after that conversation with my neighbor? I don't think so.

That's what propelled me from the financial factory on Wall Street—where we produced brand new, shiny bonds – to the small financial planning firm in Spain where I now work. It's where I can truly make a difference to PEOPLE, helping folks like my neighbor to get their financial plans running smoothly. I'm convinced that the only two items any of us really need in life are: 1) a good financial plan toward which we're making progress and 2) a daily multivitamin tablet.

As to why I chose to assist folks with their financial planning specifically in Spain, there are a few reasons. The first is that I liked that small financial district of Valencia so much that I wanted to work in finance here. *After* I eventually found a bathroom there, that is.

The second reason for choosing Spain is more obscure. It has to do with the general trend within the financial advisory business in the United States to focus ever-increasingly on high-net-worth investors. More and more, the smaller investors are moved toward some form of digital advice, like robot-advisors, and the ever-dwindling number of human advisors that service smaller clients have too many clients and are encouraged to cross-sell their firm's products to increase revenue.

I'm not onboard with that trend. Not at all. I want to help *all* investors-not just those of high-net-worth, but also those of medium-net-worth and next-to-no-net-worth. People like my neighbor (if he resided in Spain). Nor do I want to cross-sell products that my clients may not really need. So, if my morals don't fit with the direction of the U.S. financial advisory industry, it's probably best to help folks with financial advice and planning in a place like Spain.

The third reason I chose to become a financial planner within Spain is the number 95,137. That's how many financial planners are certified in the United States. Nearly one hundred thousand. That's a lot. How many of them are truly talented is a question we'll leave for another day; the sheer number ensures that there's competent assistance available for Americans in the U.S. With so many choices, odds are you can find someone good.

In Spain, on the other hand, there are currently less than a thousand financial planners who are certified. So, if I weren't in Spain to help Americans here, they may forever be lost in the woods. Or worse, trying to make sense of what an Australian financial planner tells them in English between loud sips of Foster's Lager.

Why are there so few financial planners in Spain compared to the U.S.? One reason is that the United States has a thirty-eight-year head-start in the financial planning field. The European Financial Planning Association (EFPA) of Spain certified its first financial planners in 2010. In the U.S., financial planners were first certified in 1972.

The bigger reason, though, is that Spain is an exceedingly bank-centric country. To prepare for Spain's entry into the European Union in the 1980's, several Spanish banks consolidated and merged. The purpose was to put Spanish banks like Santander and BBVA on an equal footing with the larger size and sophistication of their European rivals. The Spanish government encouraged these consolidations, and sometimes even "brokered" them. Spanish banks' quest to achieve ever-larger economies of scale was particularly important in areas where the size of a financial institution can be an advantage, such as back-office operations, information systems and asset management.

Once they reached sufficient size, the big Spanish banks had an additional growth engine unavailable to their European rivals: expansion into the large and growing banking market within Latin America. This market proved to be attractive thanks to the margins and inefficiencies of the banking systems which existed in these countries. Spanish banks came to dominate many aspects of banking in Latin America in no small part because they share a common language and culture with most countries there. Which, in turn, provided both seasoning for the senior executives of these Spanish banks as well as additional capital to grow ever larger in Europe.

The financial crisis of 2008 produced a second strong wave of bank consolidations. Savings banks in Spain were particularly vulnerable, and dozens were absorbed by more solvent banks. Currently, the three largest banks (Santander, BBVA and CaixaBank) are what remains of what had been 29 separate banks or savings banks at the start of 2008.

Independent financial planning and large banks don't often see eye-to-eye. This isn't necessarily true by-definition, but often is in practice. Many financial planners work at small- or medium-size boutique firms, or family offices, or for themselves, not at banks. Thus, given the size and importance of Spain's banks within the financial infrastructure of the country, it's not surprising that financial planning is relegated to the shadows and that there are so few financial planners.

Spain is, however, an exception to what is happening worldwide. In most other European countries, it's common for individuals to use independent advisors (Independent Financial Advisors or IFAs) for financial advice/planning.

In the U.S., independent advisors are often registered as Registered Investment Advisors (RIAs). This sector has been growing rapidly, by more than 11% annually over the past ten years. RIAs in the United States now manage more than $5 trillion in Assets Under Management ("AUM" is the industry term). Fidelity, Charles Schwab and other financial giants provide custodial services to these RIAs allowing them to serve clients at all wealth levels.

Not in Spain.

90% of the money managed in Spain is through a bank, while only 6% is through independent advice. On the other hand, in Switzerland and England, independent advice accounts for 50% and nearly 80% of money managed, respectively. So, my skills as a financial planner are of great service in Spain.

With my decision made, I set off to Spain.

# WHAT IS FINANCIAL PLANNING?

**W**HEN NEIL ARMSTRONG LANDED on the moon in 1969, how would he have reacted if he'd found other humans were already there? If instead of parking his Apollo 11 lunar vehicle in a moon crater, he'd landed in a crowded football stadium during a tailgate party? He might've jumped out of his space suit.

Well, the exact OPPOSITE happened to me landing in Spain. It turns out that I'm the first American who's certified as a financial planner here.

But I never expected to be. I wasn't selected by NASA. I merely pursued what I thought was a good idea without realizing it had never been done before.

Even after I'd gone through extensive time and effort to become accredited in Spain as a financial advisor and later a financial planner, I still hadn't learned that I was to be a pioneer. I continued to expect sooner or later to

run across an American who's certified as a financial planner in Spain gulping Starbucks coffee and talking brashly into a cellphone.

But I encountered no one.

Prior to my arrival, Brits or other English-speakers in Spain might have assisted Americans with financial advice or planning. But these non-Americans seldom know about assets an American might own back in the States (real estate, IRAs, pensions, 401Ks). I'm told by Americans here that it was like going to an auto mechanic who only knows how to fix *part* of your car. *"I can't do a thing about the fact that your brakes don't work,"* says the mechanic, wiping his hands on a rag as he explains, *"but I was able to repair your windshield wipers. When it rains, I doubt you'll be able to stop, but you'll have a good clear view through your windshield."*

What might be worse, these Americans often had to suffer through stories about Australian rules football or the British royal family just so they could get financial advice in English. Clearly not an ideal situation.

Prior to my arrival, there were also specialists who helped American expats worldwide. They might live in New York or London or California. One day they'd assist a couple living in Dubai and the next week a family in Italy. How well did these specialists know the intricacies of a country like Spain, where an American who lives there needs local advice? It's a valid question, given the great variance in laws, financial systems, and tax rules among countries. My sense is some of these "expat specialists" read from a script, inserting "Spain" from time to time in the blank-

*"As you know, Ms. Jones, [INSERT NAME OF COUNTRY] has a different method of defining a tax resident than we do in the United States. And [INSERT NAME OF COUNTRY] is also different in terms of..."*

Thus, the need for a qualified American financial planner in Spain is great.

But what *is* financial planning? What do financial planners *do*?

This book isn't homework, so let's make it easy: **financial advising** is a broad term that often includes **wealth management** (preserving and growing wealth) and **financial planning** (an approach to reach one's life goals).

If Neil Armstrong landed in Spain as a financial planner instead of on the moon as an astronaut, how might he describe the job of a *financial planner*?

To put us in the cockpit of the financial planning process, an astronaut might highlight a hypothetical couple's retirement. Retirement is often the financial goal that's the farthest away in terms of time, so it's the hardest to envision from where we're standing. Once we understand a financial planning process for retirement, we can then bring our other financial goals to the launch pad.

1. <u>The Mission. Help clients identify their dreams</u>. For our hypothetical couple, they want to retire in 2039. At that time, the husband will be 67 years-old and the wife 62 years-old.

2. <u>Planetary Exploration. Estimate the amount of money needed each year of retirement</u>. If their retirement goal is many years away, it's best to base how much they'll need each year as a percentage of what the couple is currently earning. If retirement is nearer term, it's better to calculate their future income needs starting with their current monthly budget and adding or subtracting expenses that are likely to change during retirement (see below). The number of years they'll need these monies once they retire is typically based on estimated life expectancy.

### Expenses That Could Change During Retirement

| Expenses Likely to Decrease | Expenses Likely to Increase |
| --- | --- |
| Work-related expenses (clothes, coffees) | Vacation and travel costs |
| Lower income = lower income taxes | Hobby expenses |
| Mortgage payments may end | Health care and medical expenses |
| Savings is no longer necessary | Higher costs due to inflation |
| Automobile costs are reduced, less driving | |

3. <u>Booster Rocket. Identify how much they will be receiving toward that goal</u>. Calculate what the couple should receive

each year in retirement: social security, pensions, annuities, rental property income (if they'll continue receiving rental income from that property throughout their retirement years), or other sources.

4.  <u>Black Hole. Calculate gap between income and expenses that they'll face in retirement.</u> Subtracting what they'll need in step 2 from what they'll be receiving based on step 3 sheds light on the amount their retirement income requirements will exceed their retirement income.

5.  <u>Congressional Appropriations Committee. Develop a savings plan.</u> Using the results of step 4, we look at the typical monthly flow of funds of the family. This is based on their income and style of living and gives us an estimate of their capacity to save money. Rather than abort the mission if the savings necessary to achieve their goal is unrealistically high, a more realistic savings plan is put together based on adjusted assumptions.

6.  <u>Nuclear Thermal Propulsion. Develop an investment plan.</u> Time horizons, available investment vehicles, taxes, inflation expectations and other variables all play a role in formulating the investment plan. Believe it or not, some investment advisors begin and end with this step, that's the extent of their client service.

7.  <u>Observation Satellite. Review periodically.</u> The plan is periodically reviewed. If market conditions or family conditions change, adjustments are made. If the changes are sizeable, all the steps are reviewed again. Financial plans are meant to be working documents, not doorstops or paperweights, so making periodic changes to them is natural.

These same steps would then be applied to the other goals of this couple, such as financing the education of children, purchasing a home or a second home, etc.

The goal of retirement is more involved than the goal of saving for a new car. Nevertheless, even in example above, I think you can see that you don't need to be trained by NASA to understand it.

Adding a few assumptions (inflation: 3%; earnings: 6%; life expectancy after retirement: 30 years), let's look at the numbers:

1.  46 years-old, 51 years-old.

2.  Expenses are often lower during retirement than during work years. Because this couple's desired retirement is 16 years away, a percentage of their current income, rather than their existing monthly expenditures, is likely the best starting point to estimate their income needs in retirement. This percentage is referred to as the wage replacement ratio. If the wife has a salary of $105,000/year and the husband earns $120,000/year, their combined income is currently $225,000. If they believe a 75% wage replacement ratio should meet their needs, that means that roughly $168,750 (in today's dollars) is their desired annual income during retirement.

3.  We calculate his social security beginning at age 67 ($24,450), hers at age 67 ($23,770), plus her pension starting the day she retires ($9,800 per year) and one rental property ($25,000 per year). That equals $83,020 per year. They have no annuities or other recurring income that will be forthcoming during retirement. Since she wants to retire 5 years before she starts collecting social security, (when she reaches full retirement age at 67), they'll also need to cover that shortfall. She could choose to start collecting social security earlier, not waiting until her full retirement at age 67, but this would permanently reduce her monthly social security check. This couple finds itself in the favorable circumstance of being able to retire before she'd be entitled to a full social security check but waiting until her full retirement age to collect it because they're not in need of the monies from her social security payments right away.

4.  $168,750 - $83,020 = $85,730 (annual gap). At inflation of 3%, this gap will grow to be approximately $137,571 annually when they

retire 16 years from now, in the year 2039. For their retirement savings to last to their life expectancy, the day they retire they would need the sum of $2,727,165 saved to cover those 30 years.

**Each year beginning in 2039 (plus inflation)…**

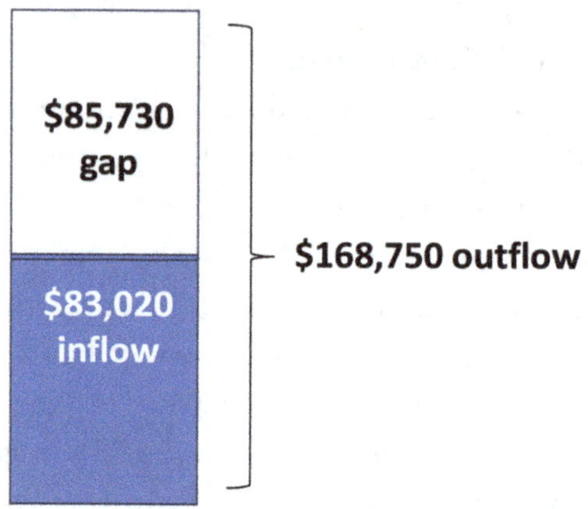


5.  If it earns 6% until the time of retirement, the sum of $2,727,165 needed in 2039 is equal to $1,073,538 today. If they have that amount already saved, terrific! If instead they have $0 saved (unlikely, though not out of the question), they would need to save about $8,711 monthly to reach their retirement goal. If the amount needed to be saved monthly between now and retirement is larger than this couple can achieve, we'd look at alternatives such as a lower wage replacement ratio or postponing retirement.

6.  Investment planning is a series of steps the planner and the client take to build an investment portfolio meant to achieve the client's goals. Writing an investment policy statement to guide the client's investment strategy is a possible first step. The financial planner provides information about the external environment, focusing on the expected economic, political, legal and tax conditions. Together, the planner and family select an investment portfolio in keeping with the investment policy statement and incorporating the expected external factors.

7.  Periodic monitoring, updating, and evaluating of investment performance is important. Updating changes in client circumstances (employment, births, etc.) is also important. The sooner the planner and client make adjustments when deviations from the initial financial plan surface, the better.

What we just looked at is just one financial planning approach, it's called the present value of goals approach.

Powerful, right? Even though it's a simplified example, it shows how helpful financial planning can be. Contrast that with the hypothetical financial advisor somewhere who buys a handful of unrelated investments for this couple and concludes, *"these are likely to earn enough to get you through your retirement years...."*

And it's important, too, it's a family's retirement dreams we've just helped them put in motion. Financial planning helps clarify what's important to a family, which in turn helps them to make better decisions.

It's why I think being a financial planner is just as exciting as being an astronaut. If not more so. Being able to assist people with the financial decisions that have an important impact on their lives is the reason I've worked hard to ensure that I can do this job well.

# INTERVIEWS AND INFORMATIONAL INTERVIEWS

**O**NCE I ARRIVED IN Spain, I hit the ground running: interviewing for jobs as well as conducting my own "informational interviews". I'm a big fan of "*What Color is your Parachute*", a book by the late Richard N. Bolles. Although it's been decades since its first publication, its ringing endorsement of informational interviews as the way to discover the ins and outs of any industry is still valid.

An informational interview is nothing more than a conversation that allows you to learn directly from people working in the field by sitting down with them, maybe sharing a coffee, and asking them what you don't know. Which, when I first began this journey, was a lot.

So, I met with financial planners and private bankers and financial advisors and finance instructors and headhunters and wealth management consultants and others in the sector. I visited with them at the Spanish offices of Swiss, French, and even Andorran banks; at advisory firms; at insurance companies; at industry events; at coffee shops; at private banking arms of Spanish banks; and at financial planning firms, traveling to Madrid, Barcelona, Valencia and Bilbao to see them.

What did I discover?

That I wasn't initially enthused about *any* of them. As I spoke to more and more people, my goal seemed to grow ever more distant.

Keep in mind that I sincerely want to help all investors, not merely high-net-worth ones. Also, cross-selling products does not appeal to me, whereas searching for the perfect product or service to fit the client's exact circumstances does appeal to me. And remember that I love financial planning, not simply investment advising – comprehensive planning is by definition more complicated and there are more steps to it, but it's far more beneficial to the client. Lastly, we haven't spoken yet about "retrocessions", but here's a spoiler: I don't agree with them.

So that's my list of "must-haves", "nice-to-haves" and "unlikely-to-finds" on the job quest.

What the industry seemed to want, in contrast, would be best summed up if they'd taken out the following ad:

# JOB OPENING

The XYZ team is currently looking for candidates to fill the position of:

## PRIVATE BANK INVESTMENT ADVISOR

**JOB DESCRIPTION:**
An Investment Advisor focused exclusively on high-net-worth clients. No financial planning involved. Pays retrocessions. Priority given to short-term results.

**REQUIRED SKILLS & ATTRIBUTES**

- **Cross selling of XYZ products**
- **Disregard for truly helping people**

Undaunted, I kept meeting with people. I visited additional firms. I asked different questions.

While interviewing with a partner at a mid-sized financial advisory firm, I explained my plan to help Americans in Spain with financial planning. His reply, which was his answer to nearly everything I said that day, *"I don't see it"*.

Him*: "Why do Americans living in Spain need financial planning help? I don't see it."*

Me: *"For the same reasons anyone would. But with the tax and regulatory complexities that confront American expats, the task is more complicated. That's even more reason to hire an American like me who's also a financial planner in Spain."*

Him*: "I don't see it. Isn't financial planning just common sense? How will you get clients to understand its value? I just don't see it."*

*Oh*, I thought to myself, *it's not me, it's financial planning he doesn't get*. So, I drew him a pie chart. Admittedly, it was crude.

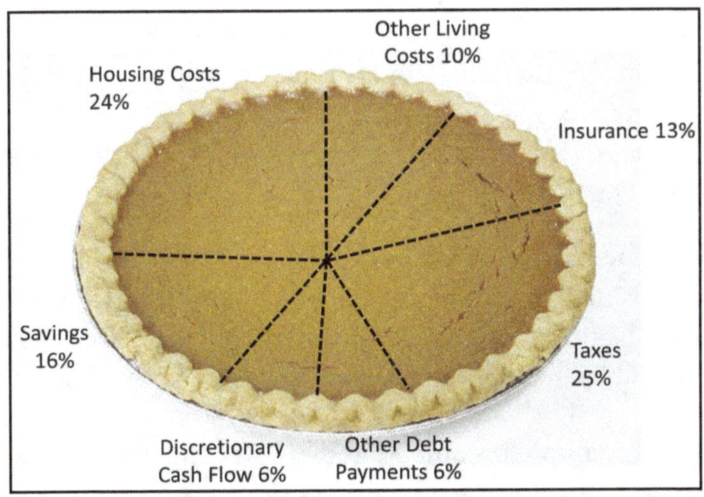


I explained that this is how I'd explain financial planning to a pastry chef. Because pie charts show a client's financial resources and how they're allocated, it's particularly suited to clients who are visual learners.

He liked that:

*"Go on"*, he said, his first words that day that hadn't mentioned an inability to see.

I told him that I'd just drawn the first of three pies, the **income statement** pie. And that it might represent a couple with gross pay of $150,000:

| | Amount | Percentage |
|---|---|---|
| Gross Income | $150,000 | 100% |
| Taxes | $37,500 | 25% |
| Savings | $24,000 | 16% |
| Insurance | $19,500 | 13% |
| Housing Costs | $36,000 | 24% |
| Other Debt Payments | $9,000 | 6% |
| Other Living Costs | $15,000 | 10% |
| Discretionary Cash Flow | $9,000 | 6% |

The income statement pie shows a pastry chef what ingredients go into his monthly budget, to clearly see the answers to these questions:

- What percentage of their gross pay is spent on principal + interest + property tax + insurance OR rent + insurance?
- What percentage of gross pay is being saved?
- What percentage goes to insurance?
- What percentage does the client pay in taxes?
- What percentage of their gross pay is left to live on (discretionary cash flow)?

The income statement pie would illustrate if maybe too much is being spent on housing, for example, which may result in under-saving. If so, the financial planner can present benchmark pie charts that show where a client should be in order to meet typical goals and objectives.

### Sample Income Statement Benchmarks

| | General Targeted Benchmark |
|---|---|
| Taxes | 15 - 30% |
| Savings | 10 – 20% |
| Insurance | 5 – 10% |
| Other living costs | 40 – 60% |
| Housing (rent or mortgage) | <28% |
| Other debt payments | <36% |

The **assets on the balance sheet** pie chart shows us at a glance what the pastry chef has in his kitchen.

Cash and cash equivalents? Investment assets? These are assets that our pie maker can utilize to make pastries in the future.

Personal use assets? These are the assets that maintain the client's lifestyle. Examples include car, furniture, clothing, collectibles (art, antiques), personal residence, vacation homes, electronics. Because many of these assets aren't as helpful for making future pastries as cash/cash equivalents and investment assets, they're often of less concern to the financial planner.

Regardless of the amount of total assets, a portion of a client's assets should be in cash and cash equivalents and some portion should be in investment assets. The percentage needed in cash and cash equivalents is related to the non-discretionary cash flows. The percentage that should be in investment assets is related to the age of the client and the client's gross income.

## Sample Balance Sheet Benchmarks by Age

| | | 20s – 30s | 40s – 50s | 60s – 70s |
|---|---|---|---|---|
| Assets | Cash & Cash Equivalents | 5 – 20% | 5 – 20% | 5 – 20% |
| | Investment Assets | 0 – 30% | 30 – 60% | 60 – 70% |
| | Personal Use Assets | 55 – 90% | 25 – 60% | 15 – 30% |
| Liabilities | Current Liabilities | 10 – 20% | 10 – 20% | 0 – 10% |
| | Long-Term Liabilities | 40 – 70% | 15 – 50% | 5 – 25% |
| Net Worth | Net Worth | 5 – 50% | 30 – 75% | 65 – 80% |

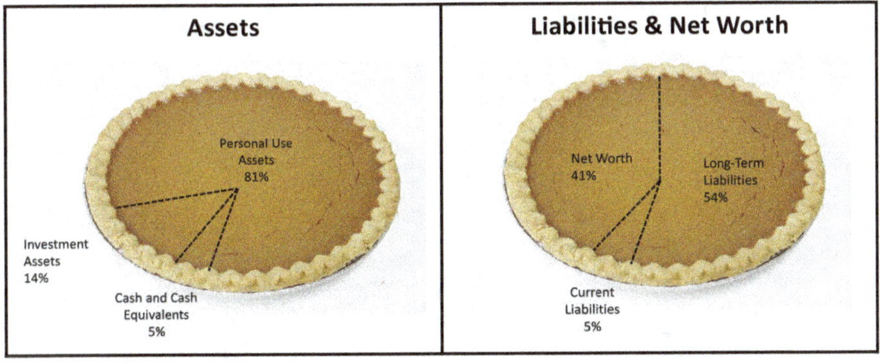

And what if our pie chef were to permanently abandon this kitchen for some reason? Not all the implements or equipment are his to take with him, or he'd need to compensate the restaurant owners for them if he did. Those are the **liabilities on the balance sheet** pie chart: current liabilities are items he'd need to replace or pay back soon after departing, whereas with long-term liabilities the restaurant would grant him more time to do so.

**Net worth on the balance sheet**? That's the kitchen appliances he takes with him that are his, they belong to him, not the restaurant.

Given a client's age, gross pay and non-discretionary cash flow characteristics, the financial planner can develop balance sheet benchmark pie charts to compare to the client's actual balance sheet pie charts. These provide an opportunity for a quick and high-level discussion of where the client is currently, and where the client should be, based on appropriate benchmarks.

These pie charts are typically used in the early stages with a client, to get a general idea of their financial situation. They don't lend themselves to detailed financial planning analysis and recommendations. They are, however, a useful depiction of where the client is at the moment.

By the time I finished explaining the three pies, my interviewer was impressed. But his firm's focus had never extended beyond giving investment advice and selling financial products. Financial planning wouldn't be able to establish a foothold there any time soon.

The question of where I should work within the financial advisory field in Spain remained a mystery.

But I kept looking…

# CHAPTER 4

# REFEREES, PLAYING FIELD, PLAYERS

## THE REFEREES

**F IT'S HELPFUL TO** know who the referees will be before we step onto the playing field, I'm happy to oblige. In Spain, it depends on whether you work for a bank or a specialized financial firm. If you work for a bank (Spanish or foreign, it doesn't matter which) related to banking functions such as loans, you'll be regulated by the Bank of Spain (*Banco de España*). If you work for a specialty finance firm (one focused on advising and managing assets), or for a bank related to their investment functions, you'll be overseen by the National Securities Market Commission – commonly known as "CNMV" (*Comisión Nacional del Mercado de Valores*).

Inevitably there's overlap between the two, depending on the products or circumstances involved, and also between these entities and the third referee-

The European Union (EU), a.k.a. the third referee, which published a legal framework for securities markets and investment intermediaries within Europe. The framework is called *Markets in Financial Instruments*

*Directive*—commonly known as "MiFID". Its latest reform is known as MiFID II. Let's think of it as the EU's attempt to insert into the game referees that have a perspective that's continent-wide instead of local. Because individual countries within the EU interpret, adopt and enforce these directives in ways that won't conflict with their existing institutional and legal infrastructures, they don't always allow these MiFID referees on the field. Even when they do, it's often not in the manner nor on the schedule that MiFID II had proposed.

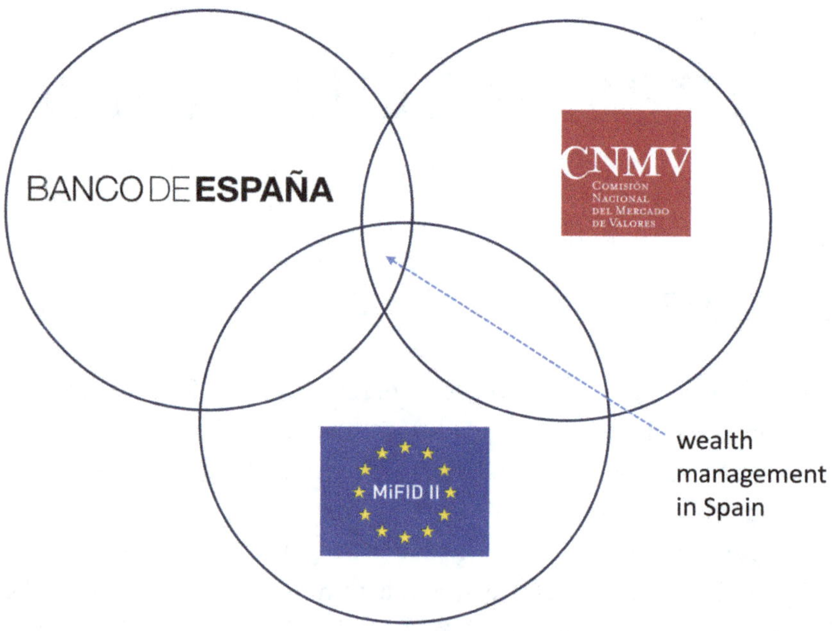


**The Bank of Spain** performs the functions of a national central bank in Spain. It's also responsible for the supervision of the Spanish banking system and of other financial intermediaries operating in Spain.

More interestingly, it's the Bank of Spain that the crooks wearing the Salvador Dali masks and red jumpsuits rob in the Netflix series "Money Heist".

**The CNMV** is the agency in charge of supervising the Spanish securities markets. It's a close equivalent to the U.S.'s Securities Exchange Commission (SEC) in many ways. Its objective is to secure the stability and transparency of the financial market. Its supervision focuses on:

- companies issuing securities to be placed publicly in the primary market
- participants in the secondary securities markets
- companies providing investment services and collective investment institutions.

**MiFID II** is the revision of the Markets in Financial Instruments Directive (MiFID I), which was originally published in 2004. It's the foundation of financial legislation for the European Union, designed to assist traders, investors, and other participants in the financial sector. Like all popular movies, its fans eagerly await the sequel: MiFID III.

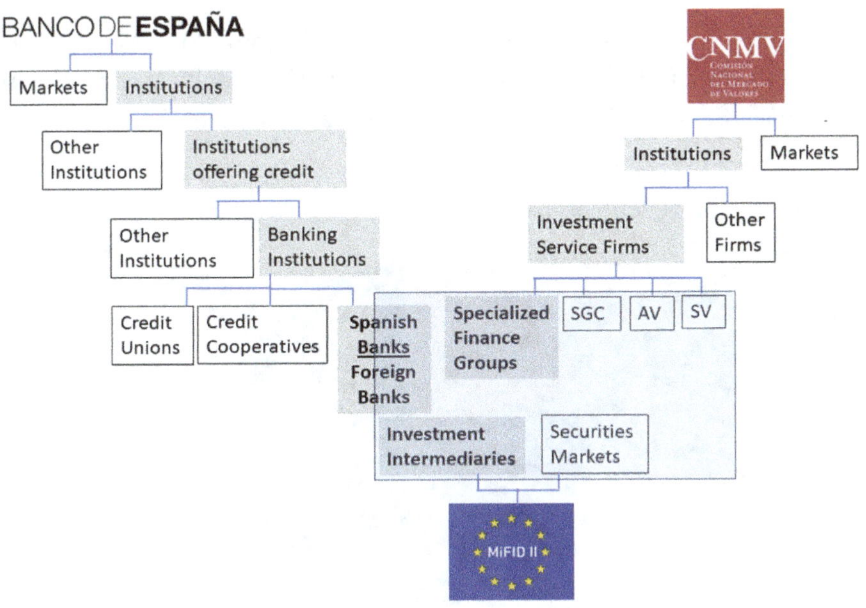

## THE PLAYING FIELD

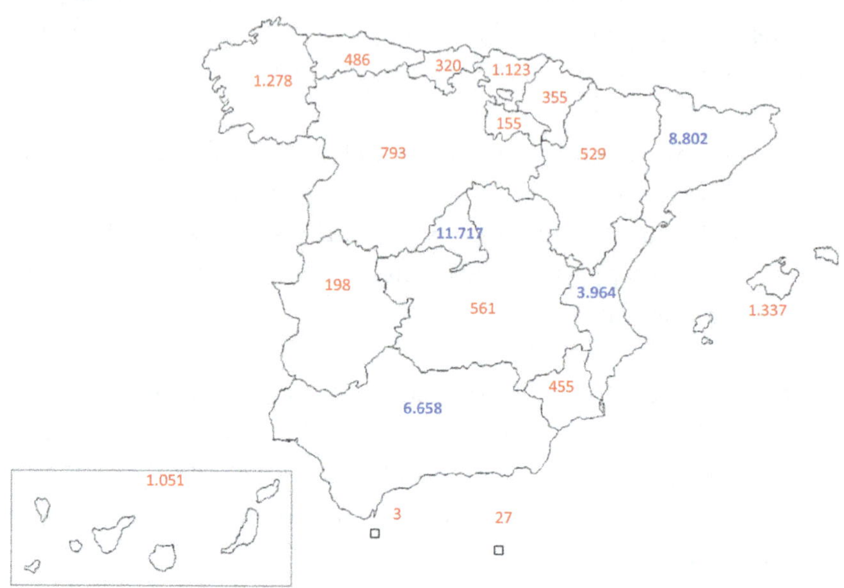


Americans living in Spain now total 39,812: 21,567 women and 18,245 men. And, although 78% live in four areas: Madrid, Catalonia (Barcelona), Andalusia (Seville, Malaga, Granada), and Valencia, there's at least a few Americans in every corner of Spain.

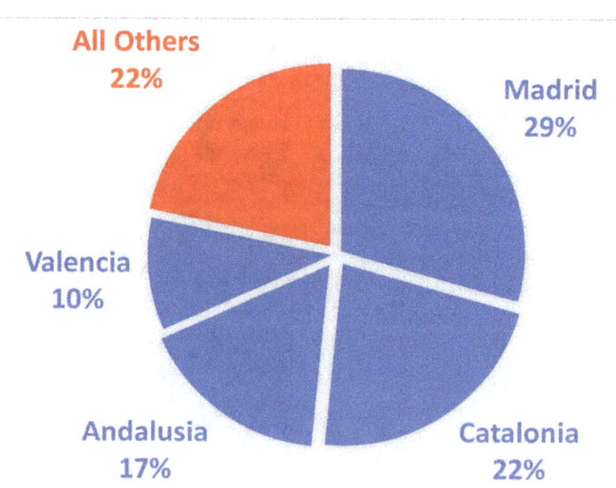

## THE PLAYERS

It's not often that we're introduced to referees and the playing field before we meet the players. But I wanted to build up some anticipation, and maybe even a smattering of applause, when I introduce Spain's financial advisory players. That's because 2022 marked the sixth consecutive year of growth in this sector in Spain. Assets under management (AUM) have grown each of those years. That this growth has taken place despite the COVID pandemic and war in the Ukraine and includes stretches where nearly all asset classes suffered losses bodes well for the Spanish financial advisory sector. Even when facing strong head winds.

Three types of financial entities make up the teams on this field: big commercial banks, specialty finance groups, and foreign banks.

### Spanish Financial Advisory Sector by Market Share

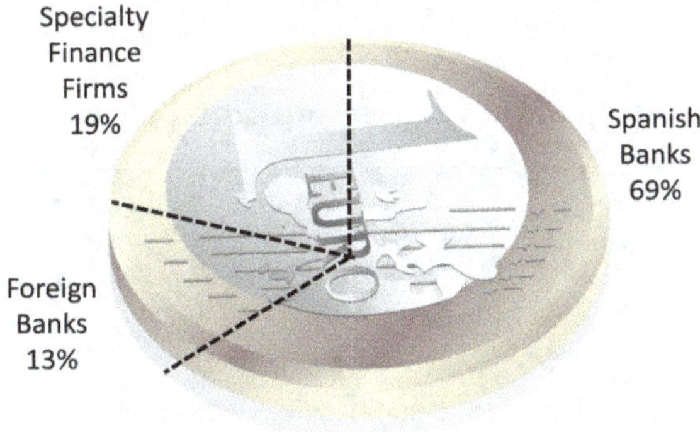


*Source: FundsPeople*

There's no doubt who would make the All-Star team if there were such a thing: the big **Spanish commercial banks**. Nearly 70% of the AUM in the sector was in the hands of these banks at the end of 2022, while **specialty financial firms** would win the "most improved player" award, having recently gained sufficient market share to leapfrog **foreign banks**, now the third largest group.

## By AUM (in billions U.S. $)

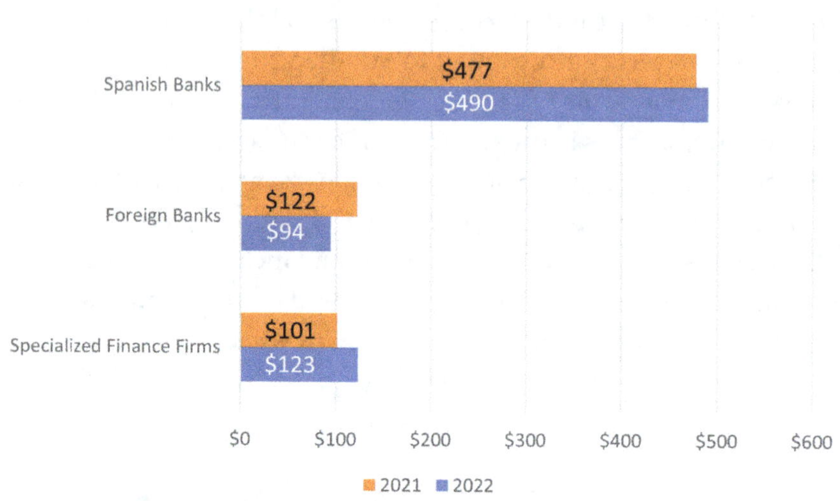


*Source: FundsPeople, converted from € to $*

## Listing of the biggest individual players:

| Financial Institution | Assets Under Management (AUM) | Category | Wealth Management Bankers | Wealth Management Offices |
|---|---|---|---|---|
| Santander | $134.248 | Spanish bank | 549 | 57 |
| CaixaBank | $125.065 | Spanish bank | 1,018 | 73 |
| BBVA | $108.281 | Spanish bank | 678 | 210 |
| Bankinter | $54.839 | Spanish bank | 210 | 46 |
| Sabadell | $34.906 | Spanish bank | 175 | 31 |
| Banca March | $25.206 | Specialty | 191 | 59 |
| Andbank | $20.170 | Foreign bank | 152 | 23 |
| Deutsche Bank | $19.307 | Foreign bank | 125 | 24 |
| Renta 4 | $17.588 | Specialty | 80 | 63 |
| Singular Bank | $14.266 | Specialty | 170 | 15 |
| A&G | $13.306 | Specialty | 92 | 12 |

*Source: FundsPeople, converted from € to $*

## SPANISH BANKS

More than half the assets managed in Spain are managed by just three large banks: Santander, CaixaBank and BBVA. If you add in the next two down on the list, Bankinter and Sabadell, you're at 65% of the market.

Spanish commercial banks have 28% of these AUM invested in traditional mutual funds (47% their own, 53% with other managers) and 4% in alternative investments.

## SPECIALTY FINANCE GROUPS

The specialized financial firm group is a diverse collection of companies that share three characteristics:

1. They're Spanish,
2. They don't belong to a commercial bank, and
3. Their business model is focused on advising and managing assets.

Included in this category are insurers who've built financial advisory groups (e.g., Mutuactivos, Mapfre Asset Management) with business models having much more in common with a private bank than with the insurance colleagues they pass in the hallway every day.

Where do they invest the $123 billion in assets they manage for their clients? Specialty finance groups have 46% invested in traditional mutual funds (32% their own, 68% with other managers).

The growth of specialized firms has been accelerated by Singular Bank's purchase of UBS Spain last year and Banca March's earlier acquisition of BNP Paribas Wealth Management of Spain, helping propel these institutions into the second largest ranking by group. Each of these acquisitions subtract market share from the third largest group, the foreign banks.

## FOREIGN BANKS

These banks make the trip to Spain from their home countries in Switzerland, the United States, Andorra, France, Germany, Great Britain and Italy. Some examples include Deutsche Bank, Julius Baer, Edmond de

Rothschild of Spain, J.P. Morgan Private Bank Spain, Banco Mediolanum, Citi Private Bank, Goldman Sachs Asset Management, Barclays, and more.

| | Specialized Finance Groups | Spanish Banks | Foreign Banks |
| --- | --- | --- | --- |
| Clients: | 100,000–120,000 | 480,000-500,000 | 35,000–50,000 |
| Bankers: | 1,300-1,500 | 3,300-3,500 | 550–700 |
| Clients/Banker: | 79 | 144 | 68 |

*Source: FundsPeople's "Private Bank Rankings"*

*Note: it remains to be seen what UBS, which signed a three-year non-compete clause as part of the sale of its operations in Spain to Singular Bank at the end of 2022, does with Credit Suisse's operations in Spain. Credit Suisse had a sizeable presence in Spain prior to its purchase by UBS in 2023.*

Thus, the question of where I should work presented all sorts of implications, from regulatory to strategic to logistical:

- Did I want to perplex potential clients by explaining that I'm an American, but I work in Spain for a bank that's headquartered in Andorra, or did I want to keep it simpler?
- Did I want to work for a financial institution large enough to have offices throughout Spain, or should I focus on assisting Americans living in just one area from a financial firm with only a regional presence? If so, which area?

- Did I want to be given a wide range of products to offer potential clients by working at a big bank on the one hand, but limited time to get to know those clients personally on the other? (Please see client per banker numbers in the trophy chart above.)
- Did I want to assist clients from one of the firms specializing in financial planning, sacrificing name recognition but gaining independence and perhaps the ability to follow my own compass?

The job *title* itself was never a concern of mine. This industry is better at coming up with new names than bartenders who concoct new drinks. The traffic jam of titles, I believe, can make us all a bit unhinged mentally: High-Net-Worth Financial Advisor, Private Client Advisory, Concierge Financial Planner, Ultra-High-Net-Worth, Prestige Client Wealth Manager, Mass Affluent, Private Banker. Even if I could tell you how these titles differ, I'd be hard-pressed to tell you why those differences matter to any of us.

Another important consideration is retrocessions, the topic I'll introduce next:

## RETROCESSIONS

Would you find it odd if your doctor never asked you to pay him? Never. And not because your insurance plan is with some happy-to-pay provider. No, not at all. Instead, it's because the pharmaceutical companies already compensate him. So, your doctor doesn't bill you. Would you trust that doctor to be truly focused on your health? Would you believe he's making his diagnoses based solely on the test results or MRI, and not influenced by which afflictions the pharmaceutical company pay him the most to treat?

I wouldn't imagine so. Yet, in much of Spain, such is the world of financial advice.

The name for it is **retrocessions**.

A *retrocession* in a standard English dictionary is *"the action of ceding territory back; e.g., the **retrocession** of Louisiana from Spain to France in 1820"*.

Investopedia, the financial dictionary says: *"**Retrocession** refers to kickbacks or other fees that asset managers pay to advisors or distributors. These payments are often done discreetly and are not disclosed to clients, although they use client funds to pay the fees."*

If there were such a thing as a 'Spanish financial advisory dictionary', this might be the entry:

> *"**Retrocessions** are how we get paid. Slang: "where our bread is buttered."*

The financial advisory world in Spain is made possible thanks to retrocessions ("retros" for short). Some folks also refer to them as "inducement payments". Essentially, it's part of a vicious cycle: Spanish bank customers often don't trust Spanish banks (sometimes for good reason, as we'll discover), and as a result they would seldom voluntarily "pay" the bank an "advisory fee" if they were aware they were doing so. It's the same reason we don't tip (much) if the service we've received is subpar.

So, most advisors in Spain "skate right over" the way they truly make money to their clients. Much as the doctor who doesn't bill patients because he gets paid directly by the pharmaceutical company might.

It's yet another reason Spaniards don't trust their own banks, which adds fuel to the fire of not wanting to compensate the bank in any way. As I said, it's a vicious cycle.

Retrocessions are paid by the asset managers, the companies that put together and subsequently sell the financial "products" that can make up much of a client's portfolio. The most common example is mutual funds. A mutual fund is simply a collection of individual stocks, bonds, or other assets that Vanguard or T. Rowe Price or Goldman Sachs Asset Management or whomever groups together under a name like "Blue Chip Growth Fund" or "U.S. Large-Cap Fund" and then sells.

With retrocessions, the client sees that within her portfolio, for example, she's gained 3.65% in her Blue Chip Growth Fund the past year. What she doesn't see is that her advisor is being paid a retro of 0.35% by the fund's managers. But because she didn't "pay" that money out directly, all turn a blind eye.

As a result, many wealth managers within Spain offer their advisory services "free" – after all, they're already being paid by the asset management or fund companies. Reliable sources tell me that 3 out of 4 Spaniards whose advisors are being paid retros don't realize this is occurring. These clients have been told that financial advice should be free so they're suspicious of advisors that want to *charge* them for advisory services rather than asking their own advisor how they make *their* money.

It's a different story entirely with an *individual* stock or bond. In those cases, the advisor does <u>not</u> receive a retro. Retros are paid only in the case of financial "products" such as mutual funds.

That's why I'd love to be a fly on the wall when a client of one of these advisors innocently asks, *"shouldn't I be invested DIRECTLY in stocks?"*

The banker might answer: *"Individual stocks are not sufficiently diversified. Mutual funds, on the other hand, are well-diversified."*

It would be as if the advisor at that Spanish bank is deliberately not finishing that sentence: *"Individual stocks are not sufficiently diversified....* as a source of income for **my** paycheck as a financial advisor."

That's how retros work. The picture gets cloudier when the regulators, the funds, the clients, the advisors, the asset managers, and the banks and other institutions with a vested interest in maintaining retros all meet on the Spanish playing field.

It doesn't help matters that I'll admit to meeting more than one slick-talking Spanish banker who can explain retros in a way that makes them sound helpful. They say things along the lines of-

*"there's two established fee structures: one where you have to go to the trouble of paying out of your own pocket and pay IVA (taxes) as well, or the other [retros] where you don't have to do anything."*

Retros sound so natural somehow when you hear these silver-tongued salespeople refer to them, as if fate somehow intended for mankind to pay via retros.

Nonetheless, in my mind, retros could compromise the impartiality of advisors and may at times represent a conflict of interest.

Further, the widespread use of retros conspires against financial planning getting a good foothold in Spain. Most everyone in the financial sector in Spain seems to know that retros are how the financial advisory machine is greased, even if most clients don't. But precisely *because* most clients don't know this, it leads them to falsely conclude that it's foolish to *pay* for financial advice or financial planning. My personal belief is it's foolish to *not pay* for such advice. And that's putting aside the reality that these clients *are* paying, it's just the way they're being billed is so roundabout that it remains hidden to them.

Thus, the NEED for good financial planners is no less in Spain than in other places, it's the DEMAND for planners that's lacking due to the current state of things.

Hasn't anyone tried to "fix" this "problem"?

There are a few obstacles which currently prevent this. First, not all would agree that it *is* a problem. Secondly, some would argue, maybe quite accurately, that the Spanish financial advisory sector has more urgent priorities for "home repair" than just retros. Also, some independent advisors have tried to bring attention to what's occurring with retros but they're small firms and are often drown out by the noise of bigger institutions.

Additionally, thanks to MiFID II, the panorama is improving. A reduced number of advisory firms in Spain can continue to call themselves "independent". And under current rules, there's now a category of clients and funds for which retros are *not* allowed to be paid. Because the advisor of such clients has discretion in *selecting*, and not merely *recommending*, the funds in this type of client account, it's recognized that it would be unfair to also allow them to accept any retros on the funds. This is referred to as the "clean" class of client and funds.

To give you a glimpse of the European Union's thoughts concerning retros, here are select excerpts from MiFID II:

*"...In order to give all relevant information to investors, it is appropriate to require investment firms providing investment advice to disclose the cost of the advice, to clarify the basis of the advice they provide, in particular the range of products they consider in providing personal recommendations to clients, whether they provide investment advice on an independent basis and whether they provide the clients with periodic assessment of the suitability of the financial instruments they recommend to them. It is also appropriate to require investment firms to explain to their clients the reasons for the advice provided to them...*

*...In order to strengthen the protection of investors and increase clarity to clients as to the service they receive, it is also appropriate to further restrict the possibility...of portfolio management to accept and retain fees, commissions or any other monetary and non-monetary benefits from third parties, and particularly from issuers or product providers. This implies that all fees, commissions and any monetary benefits paid or provided by a third party must be returned in full to the client as soon as possible after receipt of those payments by the firm and the firm should not be allowed to*

*offset any third-party payments from the fees due by the client to the firm. The client should be accurately informed about all fees, commissions and benefits the firm has received in connection with the investment service provided to the client and transferred to him. Only minor non-monetary benefits should be allowed, provided that they are clearly disclosed to the client, that they are capable of enhancing the quality of the service provided and that they could not be judged to impair the ability of investment firms to act in the best interest of their clients."*

As you can see, Spain is getting pressure from the EU to abandon retros, it's part of a push for better transparency across the board. Proposed rules for MiFID III (the "sequel") should go much further as it relates to transparency and should therefore really shake up the practice of retros.

Thus, Spaniards will realize the importance of financial planning one day. Given the way their wealth management sector currently functions, though, it won't be tomorrow. The troublesome part is that some advisors in Spain have the bulk of their clients' assets in funds that pay high retros. Many depend heavily on retrocessions for their compensation. It's a tough cycle to break.

All of this factored into my decision-making process of where to work. Clients not knowing how advisors are compensated – what in effect, they're paying – doesn't strike me as "helping" people. It seems instead like it compromises an advisor's impartiality and may even create a conflict of interest. But it's the reason most Spanish banks don't care about financial planning like I do, because explicitly charging someone for financial planning is not how they make their money. Not today, anyway.

# CHAPTER 5

# DECISIONS, DECISIONS

**N THE END, I** decided to work for a small Spanish firm focused on financial planning called BISSAN Wealth Management. I like to think of us as "Spain's plan ahead, sleep well financial experts".

Thus, I opted to ignore AUM entirely and instead use AUR as my north star. Whereas AUM is a term in widespread use in the industry to describe the amount of money managed by a given financial entity, AUR is a term I made up. But "Assistance Under the Radar" describes my desire to first and foremost assist people. Because much of the assistance I provide won't show up in any rankings or billing invoices, it'll be "under the radar". I want to *try* to be part of the solution, not the problem, on issues like transparency and retros.

BISSAN accepts clients irrespective of net worth. Whether it's medium, high, or low isn't important. What matters is that the family seeks financial planning help first and foremost, not simply assistance with investing. We'll discuss the reasons for this in Chapter 7.

BISSAN doesn't cross-sell financial products, which I like. Because it's independent of any bank, in fact, it has no products to cross-sell. I like that too. It does have three of its own funds, but these came about in response to client requests, they reduce the cost and taxes for purchases they were already making.

The question of geography didn't end up playing a role in my decision. BISSAN has offices in Barcelona and Bilbao, but because more than half of the Americans in Spain live in either Barcelona (22%) or Madrid (29%), I divide my time between those two cities. There's a saying in Spanish for this: "I'm on horseback between Barcelona and Madrid." Fortunately, it doesn't go beyond being a descriptive expression, a high-speed train connects the two cities, so horses never actually come into play.

As it relates to retros, BISSAN's policy is transparent and smart. Let me point out that a handful of specialty finance firms in Spain are categorically against the process of retros and refuse to accept them, even in those instances where a fund in their client's portfolio would ordinarily pay a retro.

That's commendable.

It's also, as I've now come to believe, a bit naïve. You might equate it to going out of our way to fail to fill in the warranty card on an expensive item you've just bought because on moralistic grounds you shouldn't ever need it. The mutual funds pay retros. Thus, buying their fund but not accepting their retros is like willingly tearing up a valuable warranty card.

The priority of financial advisers and planners, to my way of thinking, should be doing what's most beneficial to their client. Utilizing a "clean" class of funds, as we saw earlier, is one way of doing so. But for funds that are not of this type, refusing "retros" is typically not best for the client.

Returning to our earlier example, where the client gained 3.65% in her Blue Chip Growth Fund, but didn't see that her advisor was paid a retro of 0.35% by the fund's managers. If the advisor *refuses* to accept the retro, the client only receives 3.65% (if it's not a "clean" class of funds), not the 4.00% the fund would've paid out.

At BISSAN, we *accept* any retros paid on funds we've purchased for clients and *rebate* the full retro to our client. If you think about it, a ranking of the best outcome for a client looks like this:

1. Advisor accepts the retro; rebates it to client. Client receives 4.00%.
2. Advisor refuses the retro; admirable but penalizes client. Client receives only 3.65%.
3. Advisor accepts the retro. Puts it in his/her pocket. Client receives only 3.65%.

Surprisingly, BISSAN pays a big price for this policy. It's true that we rebate retros to clients, so we don't keep them. The bigger cost, though, is that only those firms that refuse to accept retros (#2 above) can call themselves "independent" financial advisory firms. So, prioritizing the client's best outcome—receiving her full 4.00% in our example above, instead of something less—and crafting a solution to bring this about works to our disadvantage: we're technically no longer classified as "independent". But no matter. BISSAN truly is independent in all the important ways: not owned by any bank, committed to offering transparent, unbiased, objective financial planning assistance.

Lastly, choosing to work for BISSAN also means I'll need to learn how to pronounce "CNMV" (*"sae en-ae em-ae oo-vae"*), the abbreviation for the National Securities Market Commission by which most Spaniards refer to it. BISSAN Wealth Management is both authorized and supervised by the CNMV (registration No. 96).

# INSURANCE, RATIOS & THE METRICS APPROACH

**NSURANCE IS A VITAL** part of financial planning because an uninsured loss could potentially thwart even the best financial plan. It takes a long time for an implemented financial plan to provide financial security for a family. Yet, a catastrophic loss or liability can occur that has the potential to upend it all in an instant.

Because insurance isn't necessary, or even available, for every risk of financial loss that a family may face, let's think of insurance as part of a broader category called "risk management". There are, in fact, numerous ways to manage risk:

- Risk avoidance
- Risk reduction
- Risk retention
- Risk transfer

Only if the client chooses to transfer a given risk and even then, only if they don't select another means of transfer (e.g., warranty), does insurance come into play.

A good financial planner uses their feel for and judgement of the family's circumstances to find the most economical and beneficial risk management tools. Typically, this includes the purchase of insurance. A review of the client's existing policies, and those they may be lacking or for which they're underinsured, should be part of this process.

The risk exposures for a family can be divided into **personal risks** where an important source of income is lost (disability, untimely death, health problems), or where the cost of living is increased (disability, health problems), **property risks** that may cause the loss of property (auto, home, or other assets), and **liability risks** that could result in financial loss (injury to a third party where it's decided that the client was financially responsible).

Insurance is available for each of these risks:

Disability – disability insurance, long term care insurance
Untimely death – life insurance
Healthcare – healthcare insurance
Property loss – homeowners'/renters' insurance, auto insurance
Liability – personal liability umbrella policy (PLUP)

One of the biggest risk management lapses in recent memory occurred in 2008 at Lehman Brothers. I worked for Lehman in its NYC world headquarters from 1995–2000, which gave me a front-row seat to the risk management system with which they successfully navigated 158 years of market ups and downs.

What caused their risk management system to fail in 2008, in my estimation, is summed up in three words- "Allan Kaplan retired".

For many years, Allan Kaplan was chairman of the firm's *Investment Banking Commitment Committee*. That's its formal name, we knew it simply as, "the Allan Kaplan Committee".

No matter what you called it, Mr. Kaplan's committee at Lehman Brothers was a clear throwback to earlier times on Wall Street; times when a firm's handful of partners met and debated whether selling a prospective or current client's stocks or bonds was a wise decision based on their collective wisdom, not the merits highlighted in a complicated algorithm produced by Google analytics. In such a conversation, they would weigh the potential pros, such as revenue to be gained, versus the confluence of potential risks if the securities didn't ultimately live up to expectations for any number of potential reasons.

Never mind that the committee now met in the corner office of a high floor of a gleaming Manhattan skyscraper, it somehow retained the feel of something old-fashioned and intimate, like a secret club to which you can't wait to tell your friends you've visited. And its purpose, although it sometimes seemed so genteel and casual, was to decide whether to approve or disapprove financings. Often large sums of money. Careers and financial fates were affected by these decisions. The stakes were high but the apparent casualness with which the committee was conducted meant that there was at the very least a thin veneer which belied that.

Times had changed. By the time I began working there in 1995, Lehman Brothers was the fourth-largest investment bank in the United States. More than a decade had passed since Lehman had ceased to be a private partnership, and it had been even longer since its days as a small, clubby firm down in lower Manhattan at 1 William Street. Instead of discussing one transaction in a meeting, like in olden times, the committee now discussed multiple potential transactions. Which made scheduling discussions of the various transactions in a day difficult.

Yet you'd never know times had changed when you had to make the case for your proposed transaction in front of the committee. Though it was less common than in earlier days for someone to smoke a cigar during the meeting, cigar smoke often lingered in the office when you walked in. And it was commonplace to see a member of the committee *chewing* on a cigar during your meeting.

We seldom witnessed other people's presentations, you'd be called by the secretary of the committee who would quietly say, "give us like 5 minutes", at which time you'd jump in the elevator and go. At times, you'd arrive before the prior act had finished, and stand outside the clear glass office walls trying to read the mood of the room to gauge ahead of time how tough your job might be that day, trying the entire time to pretend you're not looking. More than once, it was clearly tense and confrontational inside, and eventually the committee's secretary would step out to inform you, "*it might be better if you come back another time, I'll call you.*" The secretary, though not part of the discussion, had the tough role of trying to predict when to phone the next presenters to arrive.

You had to send information to the committee members via a memo a day or two prior to the meeting, but sometimes you'd never know it. That's because Allan often kicked off the meeting by saying something like:

"*Pennzoil. We like Pennzoil. Why do they need money now?*"

Or maybe:

"*Con Edison, eh? Mark and Edwin get their electricity from them. Will this transaction raise or lower their monthly electric bill?*"

And that was your cue to tell them whatever you thought would put your transaction in its best light. But not like a used car salesman. No. The committee members had bought and sold more cars in their collective lifetimes than you'd ever seen on the road. And be careful about quoting too much of the data you'd laid out for them in your memo. They had probably read it. So, if the answer to their question was already in the memo you'd sent them, odds are they wouldn't have asked. An honest, succinct summary of the facts worked best: *... good ratings from both Moody's and S&P, and although this lowers their coverage ratio, we think the revenue from this new subsidiary will offset that."*

Most curious of all was their quintessentially informal way of approving a transaction:

Allan: *"Are we okay?"*

Bill: *"yeah, I'm good."*

Sam: *"what's next on our list?"*

Allan, turning to face you: *"okay, thank you."*

And that was the cue that it was your time to leave. I'd heard of bankers over the years who hadn't read those informal signals of approval correctly and continued selling to them, only to have it backfire and lead to their proposed financing <u>not</u> being approved:

*"WAIT, did you just say that the land contract hasn't been signed? So, how is it that they've already bought equipment? They haven't, I see, they simply have an 'option' to buy equipment at that price... Well, that changes my answer."*

More than once, after getting these tacit signs that our transaction was approved, I was tempted to ask:

*"Just so we're clear, you've just given us the green light to sell these bonds, right? You're okay with the risk? Knowing that Lehman Brothers will wire out the money in the morning, and later that same day the bonds will get credited to our account, which we'll then sell to the accounts that've already placed orders for them. And you're okay with that? And, maybe just to double-check, you do realize that we're talking about $110 million, right?"*

But you didn't. Instead, you continued with the overall tone of the conversation, that this was just a friendly chat among colleagues. So, you'd say something innocuous like:

*"What's with all the construction on Vesey Street these days? I've never seen so many jackhammers in my life."* And you'd leave the room.

Idiosyncratic? Yes. They were using their wisdom and experience to calculate risk, knowing that the right risks need to be retained to successfully underwrite bonds. Yet it worked. It sometimes seemed like an anachronism, as if no one had the heart to break the news to these old gentlemen that they, and their old-world ways, were no longer relevant or necessary. But don't mistake genteelness for softness, nor polite manners for naivety. I learned more watching this committee weigh and judge risk than I can put into words, knowledge I take with me to this day.

In 2003 Allan retired for health reasons, they discontinued his committee, and he died the same year. Within five years, risk management at Lehman Brothers failed and the bank imploded. Coincidence? I think not.

## RATIOS

Ratio analysis is the process of calculating key financial ratios for a family. When results are compared to industry benchmarks, they can identify areas of risk management concern. Ratios often provide insight into underlying conditions that may not be apparent directly from reviewing the financial statements.

Ratios have been with us since long before Columbus set sail for the New World. In fact, 23% of the crew aboard Christopher Columbus' ship the *Santa Maria* were named Juan, which is nearly a three-and-a-half to Juan ratio.

$$\frac{\text{Crew members } \textbf{\textit{not}} \text{ named Juan (31)}}{\text{Crew members named Juan (9)}} = 3.44$$

There is one liquidity ratio and three debt ratios that we'll look at:

$$\textbf{Emergency Fund.}\ \frac{\text{Cash \& cash equivalents}}{\text{Monthly non-discretionary cash flows}} = 3 - 6 \text{ months}$$

The emergency fund ratio calculates the number of months a family can pay non-discretionary cash flows with current liquidity. *Discretionary* cash flows are the ones that can be avoided in the event of loss of income, *non-discretionary* are the ones that cannot. Some monthly cash flows (e.g., church contributions) may be discretionary or non-discretionary depending on the client.

| Non-Discretionary Cash Flow Examples | Discretionary Cash Flow Examples |
| --- | --- |
| Mortgage | Vacations |
| Food | Entertainment |
| Utilities | |
| Clothing | |
| Auto Maintenance | |

The risks covered by an emergency fund are those that arise from loss of employment, injury, or some other unexpected occurrence.

Here is an example for a hypothetical family:

| Ratio | Formula | | Comment | Benchmark |
| --- | --- | --- | --- | --- |
| Emergency Fund | Cash & Cash Equivalents<br>Mo. Non-Discr. Cash Flow | $10,500 = 1.47 months<br>7,157 | Very low | 3-6 months |

**Housing Ratio I.** $\dfrac{\text{Housing costs}}{\text{Gross pay}} = {<}28\%$

The purpose of the Housing Ratio I (HR I) is to calculate the percentage of gross pay that goes to pay basic housing. It does not include utilities, maintenance, or lawn care.

In general, a HR I of 28% or less is the ratio needed for first time home buyers to qualify for a "conforming" loan rate. Conforming loans typically offer lower interest rates than typical mortgages and generally require a sizeable down payment and good credit.

**Housing Ratio II.** $\dfrac{\text{Housing costs + other debt payments}}{\text{Gross pay}} = {<}36\%$

Housing ratio II (HR II) combines basic housing costs (HR I) with all other monthly debt payments. These include student loans, auto loans, bank loans, credit card payments and all other debt payments made on a recurring basis.

What's unique about HR II is the planner may need to make their own calculation of the client's credit card payments. If a client is making only minimum payments on credit cards, a good financial planner will calculate a payment using the interest rate on the card that would retire the credit card debt in 36 to 60 months, not the minimum payment the client is actually making. Otherwise, we'll underestimate the relevant ratio.

**Debt to Total Assets ratio.**  $\frac{\text{Total debt}}{\text{Total assets}}$ = depends on client age

The debt-to-total-assets ratio measures leverage. It reflects the portion of assets owned by a family that are financed by creditors. Usually, young people establishing themselves have relatively high ratios because of auto and student loans. First time home buyers generally have high ratios. Like all ratios, debt-to-total-assets is best considered over time to monitor the client's progress. This ratio is commonly as high as 80 percent for young people and as low as 10 percent or less for those near retirement age.

Here are examples of debt ratios for a hypothetical family:

| Ratio | Formula | | Comment | Benchmark |
|---|---|---|---|---|
| Housing Ratio I | Housing Costs/Gross Pay | $\frac{\$23,664}{85,000}$ = 28% | Okay | <28% |
| Housing Ratio II | Housing Costs & Other Debt/Gross Pay | $\frac{\$50,329}{85,000}$ = 59% | Very Weak | <36% |
| Debt to Total Assets | Total Debt/Total Assets | $\frac{\$344,546}{589,407}$ = 58% | Okay | Age Dependent |

## METRICS APPROACH

There's also a financial planning method that places an emphasis on a family's risk management and insurance needs. It's called the metrics approach.

If you've ever had a *nosy neighbor*, the kind who continually looks out the window to take note of what those around them are up to, the metrics approach would appeal to them. It gives nosy folks an opportunity to compare "what everyone else in the neighborhood is doing" – in this case, via quantitative benchmarks that give measurable rules of thumb of where a client's financial profile should be. This doesn't mean our neighbors are *always* right, that a family's portfolio differing from the quantitative benchmark is always wrong, but the metrics method helps highlight areas in which a financial planner should look closely and can provide important guidance.

This approach is relatively thorough and presents a step-by-step approach for the client.

| Risk Management: Personal, Property & Liability Risks | Short-Term Savings & Investments and Debt Management | Long-Term Savings & Investments |
|---|---|---|
| Check the need for and adequacy of personal insurance-<br>1) Life insurance<br>2) Liability insurance<br>3) Health insurance<br>4) Property Insurance (homeowner's, auto, other)<br>5) Long-term care insurance<br>6) Disability insurance | Check the adequacy of-<br>1) The emergency fund<br>2) The % of income spent on housing<br>3) The % of income spent on debt other than housing | Check the adequacy of-<br>1) The retirement goal<br>2) Other big funding goals<br>3) Legacy goals |

| Risk Management Data | | |
|---|---|---|
| | Metric | Comment/Recommendation |
| Life insurance | 12-16 x gross pay | Depends on need of surviving dependent(s) |
| Health insurance | Unlimited lifetime benefit | Should be guaranteed renewable |
| Disability insurance | 60-70% of gross pay >guaranteed renewable | Cover sickness & accident |
| Long-Term Care Insurance | >average for appropriate facility | Benefits inflation-adjusted Benefit period> 48 months |
| Homeowner's insurance | <full replacement value of dwelling and contents & coverage for open perils | |
| Auto insurance | <full fair market value for comprehensive and collision | |
| Liability insurance | At least $1,000,000 personal liability umbrella policy | Sufficient homeowner's and auto liability to satisfy PLUP issuer |

| Short-term savings and Investing goals | | |
|---|---|---|
| | Metric | Comment |
| Emergency fund | 3 to 6 x monthly non-discretionary cash flows | |
| Housing | <28% of gross pay | At retirement, should decline to <5% |
| Housing + debt | <36% of gross pay | |

Here are examples from a hypothetical family:

| Risk Management | Actual | vs. | Metric | Comment/Recommendations* |
|---|---|---|---|---|
| 1) Life Insurance | 29% of gross pay | | 12-16x gross pay | 1) Consider increasing to $1.5 million+ (from $25k now)** |
| 2) Health Insurance | Adequate coverage | | Complies with ACA | |
| 3) Disability Insurance | 52% of gross pay | | 60-70% of gross pay | 3) Consider increasing monthly benefit to $4,250+ (from $3,700), |
| 4) Long-Term Care Ins. | N/A | | N/A | increasing 'elimination period' from 30 days, possibly changing |
| 5) Property Insurance: | | | | 'own occupation' to 'any occupation'. |
| a) Homeowner's | Value $360k, $240k covered | | 80% replacement cost | 5) Increase Homeowner's coverage from $240,000 to $288,000+ |
| b) Auto | Adequate coverage | | State-mandated | |
| 6) Liability Insurance | None | | >$1,000,000 personal liability policy | 6) Should purchase PLUP. $1 million costs $250 premium/year |

| Short-Term Savings & Investments/Debt Management | Actual | vs. | Metric | Comment/Recommendation |
|---|---|---|---|---|
| Emergency Fund | 1.47 x monthly discretionary cash outflows | | 3-6x | Try to reduce discretionary cash outflow |
| Housing | 28% of gross pay | | < 28% of gross pay | Consider refinancing home mortgage |
| Housing and Debt | 59% of gross pay (includes credit cards, auto loans, student loans) | | <36% of gross pay | Consider reducing debt _and_ refinancing home mortgage to lower interest rates |

| Long-Term Savings & Investments | Actual | vs. | Metric | Comment/Recommendation |
|---|---|---|---|---|
| The Retirement Goal: | | | | |
| the savings rate | $8,432 | | Save 10–13% of gross pay | Consider increasing (9.92% _nearly_ meets the minimum metric) |
| investment assets | $67,647 | | Depends on age | |
| College Funding Goal* | 0 | | Save ~$3,000 per child/year | College funding needed. Consider asking grandparents to |
| Lump Sum Goals | None | | None | establish 529 plans while they are still working |
| Legacy Goals: | | | | |
| documents | None | | Basic documents | Basic documents include a will, durable healthcare power of attorney, and an advanced medical directive (living will) |

The metrics approach provides both the financial planner and clients with a methodology to achieve goals related to risks, saving, and investing. By measuring what "those around us" are doing, we get a comparison for where a client's financial profile should be. The nosy neighbor might like that.

But a *truly* nosy neighbor wouldn't be content with looking over your shoulder at your metrics report. They'd want to gossip about BISSAN Wealth Management. So, the next chapter is for them.

# CHAPTER 7

# BISSAN WEALTH MANAGEMENT

OVER TIME AT BISSAN, we've learned that the single most important factor for success when it comes to investing is *human behavior.* I'll repeat it so we're clear: our actions as human investors have a greater impact on our investing results than any other variable.

The earliest models of financial portfolio theory largely ignored human behavior. They assumed that investors are rational and went forward from there. Breakthroughs these models made might not have been possible if they hadn't set aside actual human behavior for another day. Who knows. Somewhere along the way, though, I think folks lost sight of the fact that "rational investors" had simply been an assumption, not reality. Recent investigations have conclusively shown that when it comes to investment decisions, we have a lot of biases that we bring to the table as humans, and they're far from rational ones.

BISSAN Wealth Management started helping families to invest in 2010. Shortly afterward, we began helping these and other families with financial planning. But in 2012 the Spanish stock market, where BISSAN was heavily invested at that time, suffered a cataclysmic 50% drop. Those were some very tough days in Spain, as bad as or possibly worse than the 2008 global financial crisis had been.

Curiously, the families BISSAN had initially helped with financial planning—although our approach was relatively simplistic in those early days—did not sell their investments in those moments of panic. On the other hand, the families that had merely invested with us and not received our help with financial planning, often sold at or near the market's bottoms in 2012. Human behavior in action.

The Spanish market soon recovered. So much so that by the end of 2012, BISSAN's investments were again in the black for the year.

Nonetheless, the Spanish stock market's alarming plunge proved to be a moment of clarity for BISSAN. We learned that:

- Good investment methodology can be quickly undone if our clients sell in moments of panic
- Financial planning turned out to be more important to our investing success than our own investment strategies

From that experience, we realized that assisting those clients who do not first want financial planning is not the right business model for us. And because it had been a more critical factor in investing success than our well-thought-out investment theories, we set out to dramatically improve our *financial planning* technology and process.

## PLANNING WELL ALLOWS US TO INVEST WELL.

How do people react when they learn of the BISSAN method, how it works, and the steps we incorporate in our financial planning process? "That's not something *my family* needs", some of them tell us. After all, their paycheck gets them through the upcoming week or month, they can pay for unforeseen expenditures, and they're able to save. Good financial planning, though, goes well beyond these factors: it allows us to visualize our needs, goals, and dreams for the future and to translate those into clear and understandable investment strategies. By that definition, very few of us naturally make plans based on such comprehensive factors.

And it's not because the BISSAN method is complicated (it's not—in fact, it should be and is simple and straightforward), but I'll admit it is a bit laborious, and that's why few people would adopt it intuitively. "Financial wellness" is not only about *not* having problems, but also about consistently making the best decisions.

CFOs and Treasurers are BISSAN customers. So are other financiers with extensive financial knowledge. I think this is because the financial planning process encourages thoughtfulness about one's life and finances. It's like a second opinion for many of them, an additional lens with which they can professionally view their family finances.

That even these well-schooled finance professionals would hire us shows that financial planning is useful for all types of families. It's why I'm convinced the only two items any of us really need in life are a good financial plan toward which we're making progress and a daily multivitamin tablet. The power of financial planning lies not only in the peace of mind that comes from having well-managed family finances, but also being able to obtain superior financial results.

## HOW DOES FINANCIAL PLANNING HELP US TO OBTAIN SUPERIOR FINANCIAL RESULTS? IT STARTS WITH HOW WE DEFINE "RISK".

For those in the finance field, the usual perception of risk is that it's the same as volatility. The other side of the coin is "return" of an asset, greater volatility generally means greater return. For example, owning individual stocks is risky because their prices are volatile and can suddenly fall 50%. Deposits in a savings account are not risky because they can't. And it's a workable definition for institutional investors and financial regulators and journalists. It's also workable when the time horizon of the analysis is short term. Portfolio management and risk models based on volatility and correlations of assets consider that the world ends on December 31st. If that's the situation we find ourselves in, then their approach works.

But for most individuals and families, 'volatility' is an unintentionally misguided definition of 'risk' that can lead us to invest badly, because our goals, needs, wants and wishes would have much longer time horizons.

Let's start by understanding how this all came about. Harry Markowitz won the Nobel Prize in Economics for his efficient frontier in portfolio selection. In it, he showed the optimal percentage of bonds and stocks that an investment portfolio should have to achieve the minimum possible risk (or volatility, as he defined it).

The chart below is an example of his efficient frontier with data from a one-year time horizon. At the top end of the curved (efficient frontier) line is a portfolio of 100% stocks. At the bottom of the curve is a portfolio comprised of 100% bonds. Along the vertical axis are the average returns and the horizontal axis shows the volatility (standard deviation). The minimum possible risk (standard deviation) is at 13% stocks (87% bonds):

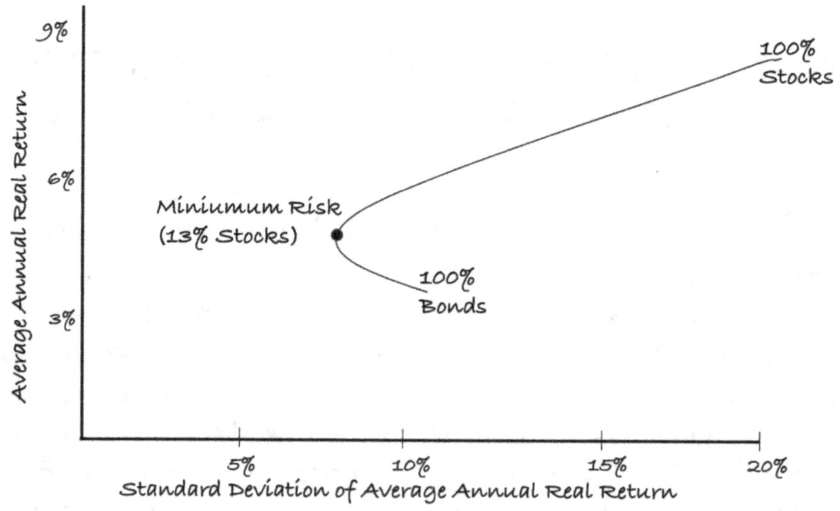


So far, so good. Just as we thought, we see that if we want more profitability, we must assume greater risk (volatility, as measured by standard deviation) and vice versa. It's an intuitive concept. It's believed by financial advisors, regulators, banks, investors, and financial journalists. But it holds true only for the institutional investor and for those who believe that the world ends on December 31 and starts again on January 1. Not for the rest of us.

If we start from the assumption that a portfolio of well-diversified stocks tends to rise in the long term (which history confirms), the paradox arises that, being volatile, the risk of loss of capital is reduced as the term of the investment is extended. From a financial planning point of view, this portfolio would be the asset with the least risk. Institutional investors, who evaluate each December 31 how much they've made on their investments, will never understand this. Our financial planning clients, however; have objectives throughout their entire life cycle—occasionally even intergenerational objectives—so thinking one year ahead does little good.

Many in the financial advisory industry (and particularly those working at banks) in Spain misunderstand this concept, too. Relying on Markowitz's efficient frontier curve and theory, the industry often segments clients by "risk profile" based on volatility and from there, the client is assigned a "target" return. (Unfortunately, financial regulators in Europe and the U.S. like using a client's risk profile based on yearly volatility when making their compliance rules).

But using this Markovitz-based profiled portfolio ignores a central factor when it comes to investing: Time. The entire theory is based on the 1-year risk-return ratio, whereas investment advisory also requires medium-, long- and very long-term return ratios.

Volatility is a discrete variable while profitability is continuous. This means that if we incorporate the time factor, returns accumulate while volatilities do not, which distorts the typical return-risk relationship. If our portfolio grew by 3.5% last year, we begin this year with our portfolio 103.5% the size as when we began last year. But if the volatility of our portfolio was 3.5% last year, that has no impact on what its volatility will be this year. The chart of the past five years illustrates this:

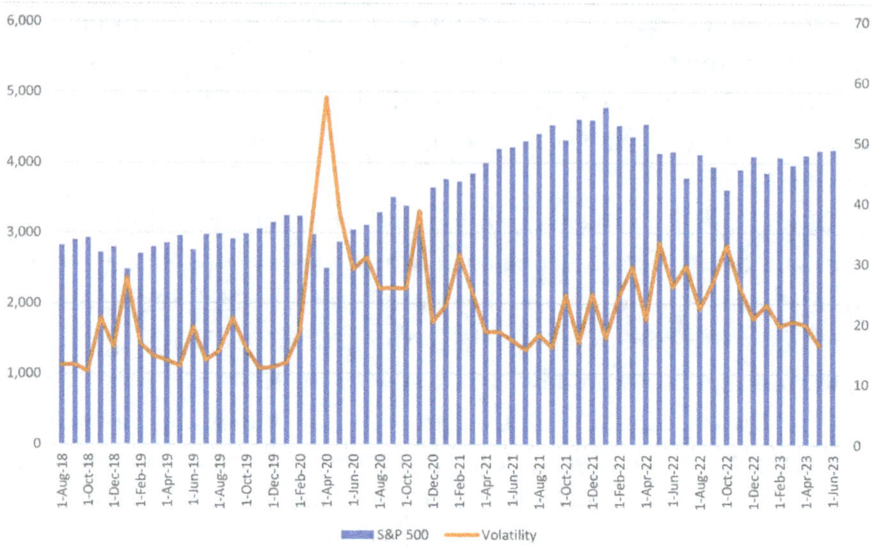


When a family determines its goals and objectives through financial planning, this time factor distortion emerges, since many of their goals and objectives are medium and long term.

As we can see in the next chart, if we incorporate the time factor in the efficient Markowitz frontier, investing for 5 years reduces the volatility at all points on the curve, yet the average returns are just as high. This is an important point to keep in mind. We also see that a portfolio 100%-invested in stocks for 5 years has significantly less volatility than for one year (and the proportion of stock held at the minimum riskiness point jumps from 13% to 25%).

And when we invest for time horizons of 30 years, the effects we saw for a 5-year time-horizon are increased: volatility diminishes further at all points on the curve while the average returns remain just as high; a 100% stock portfolio has *less* volatility than a 100% bond portfolio; and the percentage of stock at the minimum riskiness point jumps yet again, from 25% to 68%.

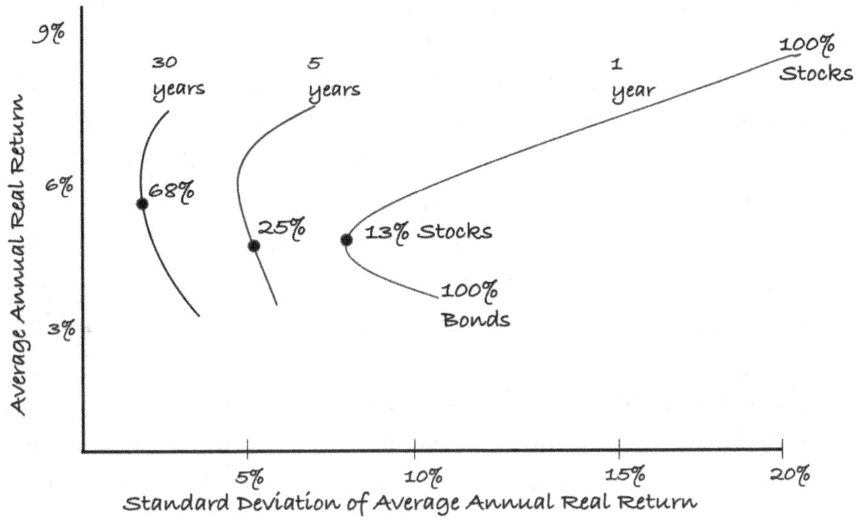


Thus, to finance our goals and objectives, our world should not start every year on January 1 and end on December 31. And that's where financial planning works its magic: we determine our future liquidity needs, the dates we need to have money in hand, in advance of our needing it. For our needs that are more than 5 years in the future, we should be comfortable investing in stocks and living with volatility, until we get closer to the actual date of the need for that money.

At BISSAN, we recognize that this runs counter to the myth that has existed in finance for years, but volatility should not be linked to risk, it is something completely normal in the markets. In fact, volatility allows us—if we have planned properly—to take advantage of market movements and have much better results than average.

The real risk to our clients is not volatility, it's that they do not have the money when they need it. In other words, not fulfilling your goals. This could be the result of the total loss of an investment, or getting carried away during a market bubble, or other factors.

So, at BISSAN we consider 'risk' as not having the money when you need it. Understanding risk in this way, and not confusing it with volatility, is the basis of the entire BISSAN method and the first step towards obtaining above-average results.

Risk equaling volatility is such a well-established and intuitive concept that getting used to this new definition will take time. At first, it's difficult to realize that even if our investments fall 25% due to a stock market correction, we shouldn't worry if we've covered all our payments for the next few years. In fact, the main risk is that we're forced to sell cheap for economic reasons (there's a crisis, and we need the money) or for psychological reasons (we can't bear the losses and therefore don't sleep at night).

I think of risk equaling volatility like a "convention" that we all agree to follow, like driving on the right side of the road. That we agree to use a certain convention doesn't mean that others wouldn't work as well, only that you're likely to be going along with the traffic pattern of others if you follow it.

So, to avoid the main risk—selling at the wrong time in the market, i.e., when it's down—it's essential from the outset to know the payments we anticipate today and many years into the future. Not anticipating these payments in advance is really risky. Whereas, if we anticipate and know them, when the value of our investments falls it simply provides an opportunity to buy. That is when BISSAN tends to invest more: in moments of crisis. We'll learn more about that in our upcoming explanation of "Dry Powder".

You may be thinking, *"but it's impossible to anticipate everything, especially in the long term."* That's true, but at BISSAN we're like a good sea captain. We have a logbook and more or less foresee what the sea will do, but the reality of the winds and storms ends up forcing us to change plans on many occasions. That's why we review our planning with clients every quarter, in order to adapt to the future, anticipating it, little by little, as much as possible.

The BISSAN method utilizes two processes to put this unique understanding of risk to use: "Guard Rails" and "Dry Powder".

# GUARD RAILS

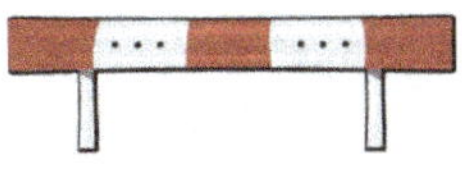 We're all familiar with guard rails on bridges and freeways. They protect us from veering off the road. In the same way, our "Guard Rails" are the measures BISSAN Wealth Management takes to ensure that our clients cover their payments for the next 5 years. They're different than the "emergency fund" used to cover expenses for 3 or 6 months if the family faces an unforeseen income interruption (as we saw in the prior chapter). Guard rails are *in addition to*, not *instead of*, emergency funds.

With guard rails, we protect the money planned for 5-year payments in very safe assets (internationally diversified deposits or very short-term fixed income) in which we do not expect to earn a higher rate than inflation. In fact, we are willing to stop earning money to be sure that our financial planning payments can be completed with complete peace of mind. It's the same theory we saw in the last chapter on insurance: we're willing to pay a premium to have money in case of need. But unlike in the case of insurance, the opportunity cost of this coverage is more than made up for by the investment in equities of the moneys that we don't need within 5 years.

The following graphs illustrate BISSAN's guard-railing process. Thanks to financial planning, we'll know the income and expenses of a family from today onward. This includes funding of the family's vital objectives (black lines below the timeline) as well as positive cash flows (green lines above the timeline) such as rents, dividends, future sale of a property, etc.

Let's start with a simple case, the purchase of a $30,000 car in 8 years:

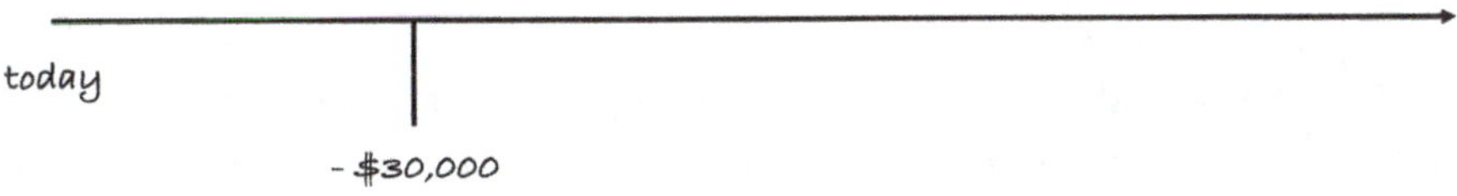

Guard-railing the car purchase will mean that 5 years before payment, we will leave money in assets with very little volatility, as shown below:

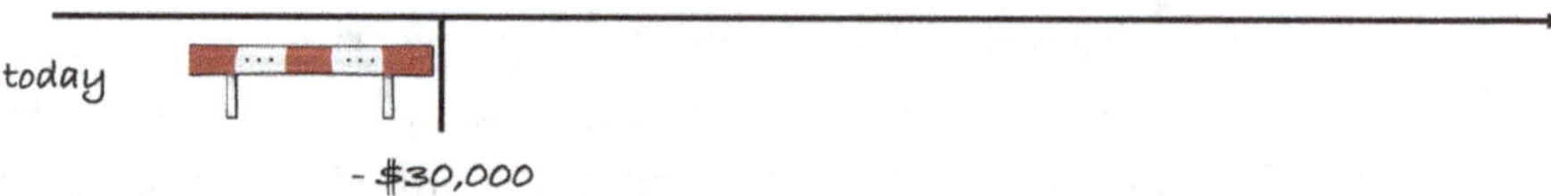


If we continue with the example, we need to know, based on the objectives of financial planning, where and how much all the income as well as the expenditures will be in the future:

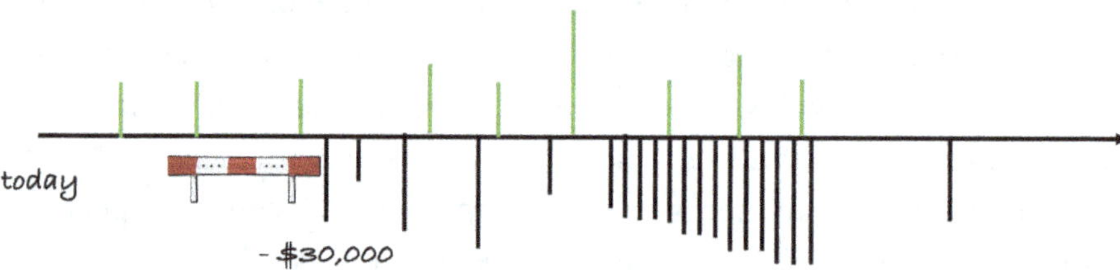


What we do is protect each of the payments before they're scheduled to occur, knowing that the money not needed for this purpose can be invested in the long term efficiently. As we see, there are times in a family's history when the guard rails of many payments will overlap. In these moments we'll need to be more cautious.

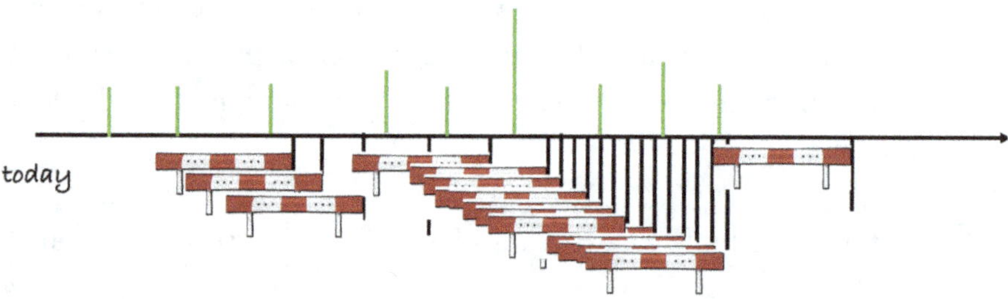


We developed an asset allocation program internally to organize and optimize these payments. We call it Cash Flow Risk Management®—risk control based on cash flows. It accomplishes the following:

- Identify outflows in terms of amount and date. Hence the importance of financial planning and its subsequent revisions.
- Five years before the date the money is needed, 100% of the required capital is invested in the money market and other short-term fixed income, so there is maximum security of having money available at the desired moment.
- If there is a payment that is due in more than 5 years, the program generally assigns 80% to equites and 20% to fixed income. This varies depending on market circumstances, though.
- In this way, the objectives are shielded from volatility five years before the date on which the money is needed, which makes the strategy very conservative.
- This makes it possible to optimize our investment in financial assets, reducing the risk of the strategy. Aggressive portfolios are built (from the market's point of view) with very little risk (from the client's point of view).

If a family has 75% of its portfolio in stocks but utilizes Cash Flow Risk Management® and guard rails for payments due within 5 years, is this risky? At BISSAN we believe that is a portfolio that generates peace of mind.

It's worth mentioning that there are at least two additional advantages to our method:

- We use a unit of measurement to which clients can easily relate: dollars. Other financial planning & investing models are based on volatility, correlation, covariance, beta, etc. When we're talking about money and not statistical regression analysis, families and the financial planner are speaking the same language and are likely to better understand one another.
- Unlike some other models, ours isn't an isolated tool that only helps with a client's "investment" assets (e.g., stocks, bonds). Because our goal is to help cover monetary expenses, the entire balance sheet of the client is incorporated for these expenses

(e.g., rents, dividends, pensions, etc.). What the BISSAN method does is include the "wealth" of a client to take better actions, and not restrict the financial plan to a client's financial assets alone.

## WHY DO WE USE 5 YEARS AS A GUARD RAIL AND NOT 3 OR 8 YEARS?

This question is key to understanding what we do with guard-railing. The entire process of planning and protection consists of the control of TIME. Most investors believe that it's important to control gains and losses. That's a very difficult task, and at the end of the day not the most important one. What almost no one does is control the time element. In a way, whoever has control of time systematically wins.

And how does that translate into 5 years of guard-railing?

The chart below shows the history since 1902 of losses that a portfolio comprised of 80% stocks and 20% bonds would have suffered. An 80/20 ratio is a very common asset allocation in families that have guard-railed all their payments. Because this graph shows only the market drops, it allows us to isolate the TIME factor. We know that in the long-run international stock markets rise. But very often they suffer strong corrections. BISSAN has analyzed these corrections to answer the question: how long will it take to return to highs after a correction in the markets?

We see that every time there was a market correction greater than -15% it took less than 5 years to return to maximums and fully recover losses, no matter what the crisis has been. The only exception? The stock market crash of 1929.

Just below the dates we see green or red lines that reflect major market corrections and the time the market was negative until reaching highs again. The green line tells us a market correction lasted less than 5 years, the red line that it lasted more than 5 years. So, for long-term investments, provided we can avoid 1929-style crashes, in less than 5 years we recover from any fall.

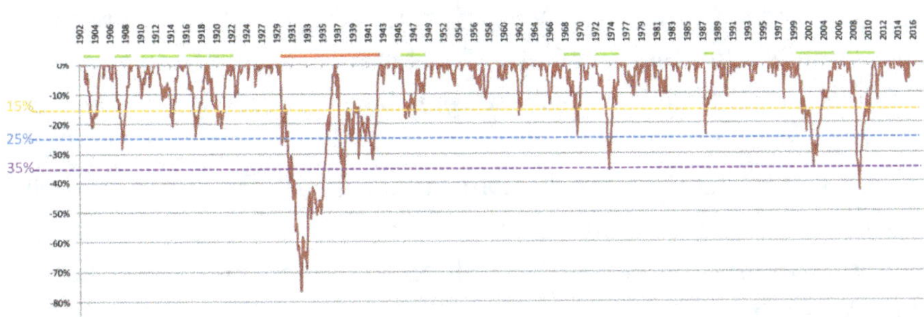



# HOW TO AVOID A CRASH LIKE THAT OF 1929?

So, other than the 1929 crash, markets fully recover losses in less than 5 years. What's the best way to avoid such crashes? Beware of speculative bubbles. It's that simple. Our task as investment advisors is to be on our guard against them. Speculative bubbles are generally characterized by the appearance of a price climax. In the final part of the bullish run, it usually pauses and suddenly starts with the greatest virulence. That's a pretty sure sign that we're near the end.

For example, in the crash of 1929, a year and a few months before the maximum, the market had grown by +100%. One thing to note is that certain stock sectors, such as technology, do have bubble behavior. But the market in general does not have bubble prices. Also, a bubble, when it bursts, implies a drop of about -75% to -95% from highs. On the other hand, corrections of -30% or -40% will often be found, but they are resolved relatively quickly (we have already seen that within a maximum of 5 years, normally much less).

# DISCIPLINE

Sometimes the stock or real estate markets get wildly bullish, and we're tempted to invest the money that we have guard-railed, or worse, the money in our emergency fund. It's human behavior, as we discussed. We need to avoid this mistake, since generally we're most tempted to invest these monies *after* big rises in the stock market or in cryptocurrencies or in real estate, which is often just *before* big corrections typically occur in those markets.

Viewed in that light, the discipline in the guard-railing process helps provide us the peace of mind to invest well. Once we have parked all the necessary money to cover guard rails and an emergency fund, then we can invest in the long term.

## LONG-TERM, THE ENGINE OF INVESTMENT

With its long-term investments, BISSAN attempts to obtain the highest return reasonably possible. We avoid both leverage and derivatives used for speculative purposes. Our financial planning is based on the fact that we will be able to generate between 3.5% and 5% annual profitability for our clients in the long term, something that we consider to be feasible. We do not need +10% or +15% annually. If that were the case, our investment plan would often fail since we would have to speculate excessively and take absurd risks, which we neither want nor need to do. You'll likely find investment advisors who obtain better results in the short-run, but BISSAN has an enviable long-term investment record.

Our long-term strategy is fundamentally designed to hold stocks, although other types of assets with strong returns in certain periods of the economic cycle are added, such as gold and raw materials, but to a lesser extent.

So, are all investments for our clients either guard-railed or invested long-term? No, there's another innovative piece to the BISSAN method. It's the small portion we always set aside, which we call "Dry Powder". It provides our clients another level of risk management—in this case, taking advantage of volatility.

# DRY POWDER

We're all familiar with the expression, "keep your powder dry". It's another way of saying: "always be prepared to take action if necessary." The expression harkens back to the days of gunpowder, which soldiers had to keep dry to be ready to fight when required. We use it to refer to another unique aspect of the BISSAN method: keeping some money on the sidelines to be strategically employed when markets fall...because markets will inevitably fall.

Dry powder is a central part of our long-term investment. Some of the assets that we invest in fixed income (think "bonds" and "money markets") in the medium and long term are put in dry powder. Being invested in fixed income, these monies can buffer some-what the negative impact of the market dips that sometimes occur. At the same time, once the market corrects, we use this dry powder to buy more shares. Thus, our clients, instead of underselling, buy with money that they've already previously planned for these occasions. The fact of having it already prepared psychologically predisposes us to see market drops as an opportunity and not as a disaster. It intelligently puts us "on the other side of the table"—when everyone sells desperately, our clients buy prudently.

Our dry powder process is a mechanism we use to execute purchases, and it has several steps depending on how severely the market falls. For drops of a certain severity, normally -15% from the last maximum, it is often activated. And we continue to employ dry powder every time a new level of market lows is reached, up to a total of three times. The last of the three would occur when market dips are greater than -35%.

**Drawdown History: 80% S&P 500 + 20% Bonds**

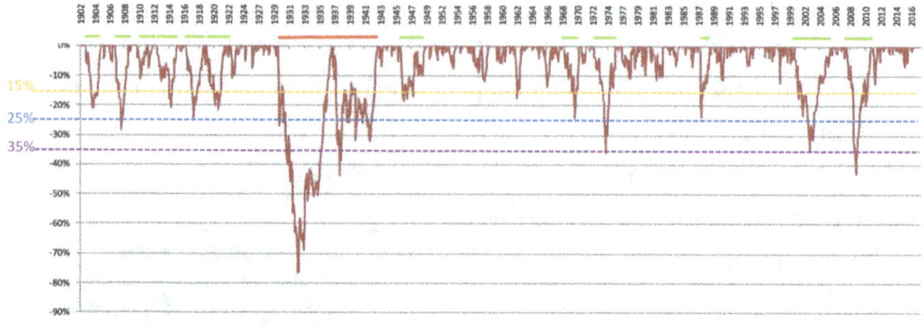

To visualize this, let's look again at the 80/20 drawdown history graph we saw earlier, adding BISSAN's dry powder process to it. We've drawn lines at 15% (yellow), 25% (blue) and 35% (purple) drops. History tells us that at these trigger points our dry powder process would have been executed every 4 years or so, more or less. The dry powder process is executed based on the prices set by the indices, not on what each client holds. BISSAN does this because it's the market, as a whole, which determines the moments of purchase, since it issues clearer signals. For example, sometimes the dips in our clients' portfolios are less than the market's dip, nonetheless, we still buy as part of the dry powder process because it's worth doing. Sometimes our portfolios fall more than the market, but it's not convenient to anticipate. For the dry powder process, we let the market guide us.

We've automated our dry powder process, but only up to a point. BISSAN's investment team monitors markets around the globe, so at those times there's meaningful disparity between markets, it's something of a judgment call. If the S&P 500 drops only 12% but the Eurostox 500 drops 18%, is dry powder triggered? It would depend on several factors: conditions in other assets, other markets, etc. So, these 15%, 25% and 35% drop triggers relate to a "basket of market indices" and not just one.

## BISSAN INVESTMENT METHODOLOGY.

Our starting point is that investing isn't about "putting our money to work", it's about asking ourselves what objectives we'd like this money to help us achieve. Because our investment recommendations come only *after* we've completed a thorough financial plan, not *before*, we're able to select investments that best fit a client's state of affairs, whether that's bonds, individual stocks, funds, etc.

Only after we've analyzed our client's balance sheet, income statement and objectives, can we know how to invest a client's financial assets. We provide a diagnosis of our client's finances and draw up a budget to see what is going to happen in the future based on our current decisions. Obviously, the future will never be exactly as we think. But this allows us to clearly understand the possible scenarios to make the best possible decisions and adapt at all times to changes and unforeseen events.

It's important for decision-making to know, month by month, what a family *should* have to meet its goals and what it *does* have in assets. Everyone is different. The circumstances and the global vision are key to making optimal decisions. Every quarter we send a periodic review report that incorporates a view of each client's global wealth. This information—financial assets of all kinds, real estate, companies, homes and debts—is updated monthly. It illustrates both the budget of the family and the real valuation of their assets, the "theory" vs. the "reality".

# CHAPTER 8

# PENCILS DOWN!

**A**M I THE ONLY American who's an accredited financial planner in Spain? We're 99.99% certain. I have yet to hear of, meet, or stumble across another one. And I've looked.

In fact, Spain's European Financial Planning Association's branch, which sets the standards for financial advisors and financial planners in all of Spain, lists only two European Financial Planners (EFPs) with less than 3 names: Zhana Fenenko and Peter Dougherty.

EFPA Spain plays a significant role nationally because the Spanish financial sector relies on self-regulation. EFPA bestows the EFP, EFA, EIP and the EIA certifications, which admittedly is a lot of similar-sounding credentials. *"Haven't they ever watched* Wheel of Fortune?*"* I wondered when I first learned about the credentials they grant. *"Don't they realize there are other letters in the alphabet?"*

As you can see, EFP (European Financial Planner) is at the top of EFPA Spain's pyramid, but a requisite for being able to enroll in its test is that one must first become a EFA (European Financial Advisor).

## EFPA Spain Certifications

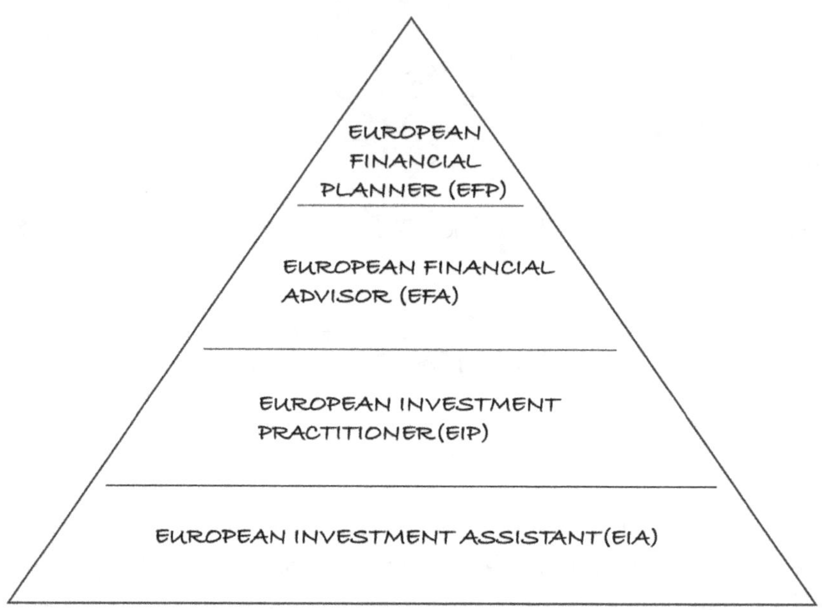


Also, is it just me, or do 'EIP' and 'EIA', somehow conjure up the song- *Old MacDonald had a farm*?

*"EFPA España had an exam,*
*E I E I A,*

*And on that exam, it had ques-tions,*
*E I E I P..."*

So, I registered for the EFA exam. It's a 2 ½ hour test that's offered four times per year in various cities. Like about 70 others that day, I chose to take it in Madrid.

December 13, 2019 –Economic Science and
Business Management building, Autonomous University of Madrid.


*"Fill in your National Identification Number, or if any of you happen to be foreigners, your European passport number, in the blank squares at the top of each of your answer sheets..."* broadcasts the test proctor loudly as we get settled to take the Financial Advisor exam, *"...and you can start your test NOW!"*

I quickly raise my hand.

*"I'm a foreigner, but my passport isn't European,"* I explain to her, *"so there's too few numbers to fill in all the spaces provided."*

She strides over to where I'm seated to get a firsthand look at my documents. *"This is an AMERICAN passport!"* she exclaims, expressing a sense of bewilderment that I was ever allowed in the testing room. She asks for my troublesome passport, says something about- *"needing to talk to her supervisors"*, and quickly disappears behind a door.

Eight minutes pass, according to the clock on the wall, but our test proctor hasn't returned. I wonder if I'll ever get my answer sheet back. Or my passport. And if so, will the exam be over by then? Meanwhile, those around me have already lost interest in my delay and begun their test: calculating, flipping pages, fidgeting, scribbling.

I grow nervous. At the nine-minute mark, the test proctor starts to enter the room again. But she's just as quickly pulled back out by someone, apparently the weighty matter of how to identify myself on the answer sheet requires further discussion.

The exams are taken with pen and paper. Although the answer sheets appear as if they could be quickly scanned, graded, and tabulated by computer, they can't. Because most of the exam consists of written case studies, which need to be corrected by hand, even the multiple-choice questions are graded by hand. So, to prevent favoritism or bias, no test takers' names are written on the answer sheets, only ID numbers.

Finally, the proctor returns to the room with my answer sheets and passport in hand. She explains to me that how I was to be identified on the answer sheets needed to go "all the way to the top" (wherever that is). I see that in the collective wisdom of "those at the top", the solution was to write "USA", together with my passport number and my name in bold letters across the top of every answer sheet. So much for anonymity.

I begin the test. It's all in Spanish. That's not a surprise. I take a moment to acknowledge how far I've come since first studying Spanish back in the day. But I don't linger. It's a self-selected group of test-takers— no one wanders into this exam without a great deal of preparation—yet the pass rate is typically less than 70%. And I'm starting my test late due to the time those "all the way at the top" chewed up deciding how to identify the answer sheet of an American.

Truthfully, I enjoy this stuff, so I hunkered down and gleefully completed my test.

As I handed my answer sheet to the test proctor, I was strongly tempted to pull her leg by saying: *"I had no idea this test would be in Spanish! I left the entire answer sheet blank!"*

But I didn't. One never knows who's going to be grading your test.

There's also a divide between American and Spanish humor. Some of the funniest things I think I've ever said to a Spaniard – believing that I simultaneously nailed the timing, and the translation and the punchline just perfectly – were met with a blank stare. And maybe a comment like, *"oh, that's interesting, I never knew that."* It's not that Spaniards don't have a good sense of humor, they often do. It's simply that it's different than American humor.

So, instead of joking, I thank her for helping get my answer sheet problem sorted out so quickly (which is a private joke just to myself) and depart.

Three weeks later, the news arrives that I've passed. Actual scores are never assigned, either the European Financial Planning Association of Spain congratulates you on passing…OR…well, I've been fortunate enough to never learn what happens if you don't pass an EFPA Spain exam.

Great. Now I'm one of about 17,000 accredited financial advisors in Spain. What I learned while studying for the EFA is both interesting and helpful, and it's a valuable credential. My development, however, wouldn't stop there. As I mentioned earlier, I think having a financial plan that we're making progress toward and taking a multivitamin tablet each day are the two items we can't do without in life. So, my understanding financial *advising* in Spain is a step toward understanding financial *planning* here, not the destination.

But the EFP (European Financial Planner) exam is a tough mountain to climb. To provide some perspective, although no one accidentally walks into the EFA exam room, only prepared candidates, there's typically a less than 70% pass rate. To register for EFP exam, you must *already* be an EFA in good standing with EFPA Spain. Even still, typically the EFP has a *less than 70% pass rate*.

Sorry, I realize that trying to keep EFA and EFP separate is a headache waiting to happen. Let's see if EFPA's definition of the two distinct certifications helps us:

European Financial Advisor (EFA) – *Comprehensive practice of financial advice. Refers to professionals who offer a rigorous service of assessing clients' needs and developing financial solutions, particularly concerning investments at portfolio level, but also including basic insurance/retirement /credit/financing solutions.*

European Financial Planner (EFP)- *Integrated practice of financial planning including investments at portfolio level, estate planning, international taxation, retirement, and insurance needs not only for private clients but also for business owners.*

No, that doesn't clear up much of anything. So, let's leave EFA in our rear-view mirror and fast-forward to the EFP exam.

———

July 9, 2021. European Financial Planner of Spain exam. EFPA Spain had cancelled the two tests prior to ours because of COVID 19, so our exam was unique in many ways, but not in its difficulty. Just as pre-COVID, it consisted of 4 hours of complex case studies and two hours to race through 50 multiple choice questions: six frantic hours total.

The exam is typically held on a college campus. But due to the pandemic, our test was held inside a hotel conference room. And we were required to wear a COVID mask the entire time: all six hours. It was a sweltering 92 degrees in Madrid that July day, with high humidity, but our masks stayed on.

The hotel conference room was the perfect size to accommodate the 30 of us who nervously waited to take the exam. We'd all put in a lot of work studying and preparing and our fate would be decided by how well we performed over the course of the next six hours. Ordinarily it would be a benefit that the room has no windows, no distracting views of the outside world during the exam. But the air-conditioning in our conference room didn't work that day. Having no windows meant that there was no relief of any kind, though I'm not sure opening a window to a 92-degree humid day is of much help.

What there was instead, however, was an uninterrupted string of hotel workmen and employees knocking on our door during our exam to announce, *"I hear your air-conditioning isn't working! Mind if I take a look?"* They'd then walk into the conference room, tinker with a few dials or even clamber on top of a table or two, and then depart without having fixed anything. A few minutes later, a different technician would knock on the door and repeat the process.

I'll never know if our exam proctor was counting his steps that day. With the sheer number of times he had to get up from his desk to let yet another workman look at the non-working air-conditioner, it wouldn't surprise me if he shattered his personal daily 'steps' record. I can imagine him arriving home that evening, soaking his aching feet and explaining to his family that proctoring an exam involves a lot less sitting than it used to. Despite the countless technicians for whom he opened the door that day, they could never get the air-conditioner to work.

At one point, a group of well-intentioned hotel employees wheel a large electric fan into our conference room. Where they found it, I'll never know, but they had to enter through the double-doors on the side of the room and move tables aside just to accommodate its width. Despite anticipation that the fan would instantly transform the conference room from a sticky swamp into a comfortable oasis, when they turned it on, it failed to do anything but scatter test papers from nearby tables and produce a loud scraping noise. Something metal had apparently broken off inside the fan's interior. So, they quickly unplugged the big fan and wheeled it back to whatever airplane hangar or oversized warehouse from which they'd first dug it up. And they completely gave up on ever cooling the sweltering room.

But I hardly noticed. You may have by now realized that I really enjoy financial planning. So, the opportunity to work through six hours of calculations and tax implications and theory and cases was what I was happily focused on, not on the conditions of the room.

Nor was I concerned with how little Spain's laws and taxes have in common with U.S. laws and taxes. Oddly, I was preoccupied with a minor detail in the matrimony-law section. Catalonia has separation of assets, and all the other regions are governed by community-property rules. In the sample tests I took to prepare for the exam, questions would name an obscure town in which the couple was first married or to which they'd subsequently moved. I knew the applicable Spanish law, what I didn't know, as I worked my way through sample tests, was whether that town was in Catalonia or not. I'm sure it's not something the folks who sat down and designed the test ever thought of; how were they to know an AMERICAN, who doesn't know which towns are where, would one day take their test? I went so far as to spend time looking at a map of towns in Catalonia, reasoning that if I knew them and a town appeared on the exam that I didn't know, then it must be in a community property community. As it turns out, none of those questions appeared on the test.

Once again, a few anxious weeks later, the news arrives that I've passed. Once again, no score is included.

If I make myself out to be like some lone gunslinger in a Western movie who shows up in Madrid one day to sit for the rigorous EFP exam, I'm not. I was boosted by the education I received at the Fikai School of Finance (*Fikai Escuela de Finanzas*) in Bilbao. To help with my test preparation, I'd enrolled in their combined online + in-person EFP course, which took place via a series of videocalls because of COVID 19. I received much more than I bargained for: the instructors at Fikai helped me develop financial planning tools that go well beyond those needed for the EFP exam.

The Fikai School of Finance, run by Juan A. Santos and his son Jon Santos, offers financial certification programs, continuing education, specialized programs and more. The quality of their coursework and instructors is second-to-none.

Germán Guevera, EFP, coordinates Fikai's European Financial Planning program. A bonus for those of us in the course is that both Germán and Juan A. Santos (who also holds the EFP certification) *teach* classes in the program. Finally, let me acknowledge the helpful Zoom classes taught by Ana Campos, Javier Serna and my friend Sergio Miguez. Many thanks, Fikai team!

# CHAPTER 9

# AMERICANS IN SPAIN

**W**HEN IT COMES TO their finances, it's as if Americans in Spain own three pairs of shoes—a Spanish shoe and an American shoe in every pair. Sadly, one shoe was manufactured in one factory and its mate was manufactured in a different factory. And the two factories don't measure or manufacture shoes in the same way. So, they don't look good if someone wears them together. Which is precisely what Americans in Spain do.

As if that weren't enough, *neither* shoe fits too well. Neither the right shoe nor the left shoe. An American in Spain might try on the right shoe, and it may be oversized. Then they try the left one and they can barely squeeze their foot into it, an even worse fit than the right. It's the same in all three shoeboxes:

- Taxes
- Investments
- Financial Institutions

Unfortunately, these are the shoes available. No refunds or exchanges. You need to wear them or go barefoot. There's no alternative option like the one suggested in an old joke:

A blonde went to buy new shoes.

The shopkeeper told her the new shoes may feel a bit uncomfortable the first couple of days.

Blonde: *"Alright. I'll start wearing them on the third day."*

Let's begin our discussion with the TAXES shoebox:

## TAXES

The U.S. is unique. It's the only country fully committed to "citizen-based taxation": subjecting its citizens to income tax on their worldwide income regardless of where they live. In other countries, you have no tax obligation to your home country if you haven't been living in it for a few years.

*Note: the east African nation of Eritrea also taxes its citizens outside the country, but at a low flat rate. I'd never heard of Eritrea before learning this, so let's call the United States the only major country that does this. My apologies, Eritrea.*

Maybe the United States does this because it has the administrative capacity and power to enforce worldwide taxation of its citizens. Or maybe it's too deeply entrenched in the history of the U.S. for the nation to ever change. It started back in 1861, as the U.S. struggled to raise revenue for the Civil War: Congress imposed a tax on personal income of 3% on all incomes greater than $800. At that time, Congress argued that American citizens living outside the country were avoiding their duties to their country in a time of need. They reasoned that those citizens could make up for their lack of civic engagement by paying a higher tax on their income emanating from the United States. So, the first federal income tax legislation ever put into place in the U.S. put individuals living abroad at a disadvantage. Soon thereafter they were required to pay taxes on their worldwide income and not just on their income in the United States.

Eventually the U.S. instituted a foreign tax credit, to eliminate the issue of double taxation for Americans overseas. Foreign tax credits are intended to relieve taxpayers of the double tax burden of income earned abroad being taxed by both the United States and the foreign country. This credit reduces the U.S. tax that an American in Spain would pay on their income earned in Spain but would not reduce U.S. taxes on income earned within the States. The foreign tax credit is an IRS rule, it's not based on any tax treaty that exists between the United States and any other country.

The foreign tax credit, however, highlights the stark mismatch that exists between the American and the Spanish Taxation shoes. As it relates to tax treatment of mutual fund sales, for example, Spanish tax law allows an investor to remove their money from one fund and place it in another without tax consequences. It allows not only tax-free switching of funds within a mutual fund family, but also from one fund family to another, and even from certain types of savings plans to mutual funds. These transfers would be subject to U.S. taxes because there's no equivalent U.S. mutual fund transfer rule. Thus, there's no foreign tax credit available those years the transfers occur because there's no tax on the Spanish side but there is tax on the U.S. side. In the year when those fund assets are finally sold, and not merely placed into a different fund, the big tax bill comes due in Spain. So, in the year there would be a big foreign tax credit available on the American tax side, it's of little benefit because—by having been already taxed every time there was an exchange—there's little U.S. tax due that year.

If, for example, in the second year of holding Fund A in her portfolio, an American in Spain were to transfer the money to Fund B, and then again from Fund B to Fund C in year 3, and to eventually sell Fund C in year 6, the foreign tax credit effects would look like this:

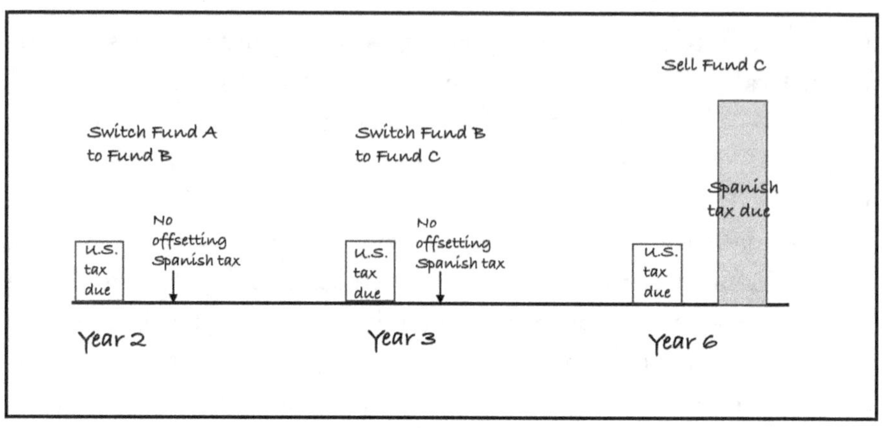


*Note: Fortunately, foreign tax credits can be carried forward for up to 10 years, so there may be an opportunity to utilize some of those credits on U.S. taxes in future years.*

In 1924, an American who had lived in Mexico for more than 20 years and no longer had ties to the U.S. brought a case to the Supreme Court, arguing that it was unconstitutional for the U.S. to continue to tax him. The court didn't agree, ruling that "citizen-based" taxation was constitutional. The Supreme Court's justification was no longer about duty to his country, but about the "inherent benefits" that came from being a citizen.

Not long after that trial, the U.S. government introduced the Foreign Earned Income Exclusion (FEIE), trying to solve the problem from a different angle. The FEIE allows taxpayers to exclude an amount of foreign-earned income from U.S. taxation. It's the other method the IRS provides for Americans living abroad to avoid double taxation on their income earned overseas. The assumption is that because the expat is already being taxed in the country in which they reside on income earned in that country, they can *exclude* that income (currently up to about $120,000) from American taxation if they qualify. However, the FEIE does not apply to passive income, such as interest paid on bonds or dividends paid on stock in Spain. There are two tests, either of which can be used to determine if an expat can qualify for the exclusion: the Physical

Presence Test or the Bona Fide Residence Test. Both tests stipulate "to pass this test, ALL of the following must be true", so passing either test is not too altogether different from passing a high school Algebra test: if you have the right answers at hand, you'll do fine. If an expat qualifies for the FEIE, it's sometimes advantageous to use it. If they don't qualify, foreign tax credits are typically the next best alternative. But this depends on an individual's circumstances.

Since the introduction of the Foreign Earned Income Exemption, discussion about the taxation of nonresidents has centered around the FEIE and foreign tax credits. Nothing more has been said about abandoning citizen-based taxation.

All of which means that an American in Spain cannot discard her American taxation shoe. No matter how badly it fits nor how long she's lived outside the U.S. She still needs to submit a U.S. tax filing every year. Her only viable alternative to doing so is to throw the shoe out the window and renounce her American citizenship. That's a drastic step involving serious, permanent, and often unintended consequences. As we'll soon see as other IRS rules enter our discussion, though, being forever free of IRS rules because one is no longer a U.S. citizen can sometimes appear to be an answer from the heavens.

So much for the American TAXES shoe, the one you can't ever discard.

The Spanish TAXES shoe doesn't fit too comfortably either. Spain does not have "citizen-based" taxation like the United States. In Spain, whether you're a tax-resident depends on if you spend more than half the year (183 days) in Spain or if your major source of income or economic activity is within the country. Even if neither of those tests is met, you'll still be considered a tax-resident if your spouse or dependent children live in Spain. In this case, you'll likely be taxed on your global holdings.

If an American has less interaction with Spain than that, spending less than 183 days, does not have significant Spanish business interests nor income, and does not have a spouse or dependent children living there, they'll likely qualify to pay non-resident taxes. Taxes for non-residents are typically lower and less complicated than that of tax-residents. In addition, only your domestic holdings within Spain will be taxed.

Some special more-favorable tax regimes such as the Beckham Law also exist for those who qualify.

Income taxes for those folks considered Spanish tax-residents are typically higher than equivalent taxes in the U.S. The process to calculate income tax in Spain also has some differences: income received from work-related activities is kept separate from income produced from savings/investments and a different tax rate is applied to each.

Despite the many incompatibilities that exist between the income tax rules and procedures of the two countries, they share, in my opinion, an overemphasis on the exceptions and special circumstances instead of a description of the general procedures. Here's an example from one of my U.S. taxation textbooks: …however, in the event…unless that asset is put in place…but not before… only in the same tax year…, not including those…, unless the deadline…nevertheless, whenever…except when…".

More than once, while reading descriptions of these complicated special tax circumstances, I've had to look back at the chapter heading to remind myself of what the topic is: *Is that sentence referring to the exception or the exception to the exception...*", I think to myself, "*...or something else entirely?*"

My Spanish taxation textbooks aren't any better.

Just as with taxes in every country around the globe, Spain's tax system has its idiosyncrasies. As in the U.S., history plays a role. Spain emerged from its civil war in 1939 with sizeable economic problems. The war's devastation had reduced the productive capacity of the country's agriculture and industry, gold and foreign exchange reserves had been virtually wiped out and the outbreak of World War II rendered many needed supplies unavailable. Recovery was slow and wasn't made any easier by Spain's large, corrupt, and inefficient bureaucracy. Tax evasion was chronic. Franco instituted a 12% income tax rate. However, income tax on wages earned on a second job was 0%. I have yet to learn whether the ideological tradition in Spain of having sources of income that aren't taxed was born at that moment or whether this was simply a continuation of earlier predispositions to do so. In either case, we know that many people claimed to have second jobs not subject to an income tax after that. Not surprising. The idea of keeping a "second set of books" seems to be ingrained in the Spanish psyche.

All of this may help explain why the local Spanish tax inspector has much more authority and autonomy than an IRS agent in the U.S. Historically, part of their role was to discover not if but *how* the taxpayer was evading taxes, to look for that "second set of books". Further, unlike in the U.S., Spanish taxation has no case law, so there's not a set of established past rulings to look to that would provide boundaries to assist these Spanish tax inspectors in rendering their decisions.

Those aspects of the Spanish TAXES shoe are curious but not particularly troubling. Far more ill-fitting is that Spain has a "wealth tax".

The concept behind a wealth tax is like a real property tax. You're probably familiar with the idea of a property tax, to help finance local school districts, etc. A wealth tax, instead of taxing only real estate, covers *all* wealth that an individual owns. And the Spanish wealth tax applies to both tax-residents (who pay based on their worldwide assets) and non-resident taxpayers (who pay based on their Spanish assets only).

The Spanish wealth tax was first introduced in 1978 as an emergency measure. It was later suppressed for a time but was reintroduced in the aftermath of the global financial crisis of 2008. The financial crisis burst what had until that time been a Spanish property bubble, provoking a property crash. Construction collapsed, unemployment spiked, and a recession ensued. This downward economic spiral lasted much longer than in many other countries.

Now that the financial crisis is a distant memory and Spain's economy has improved, various attempts to suspend or repeal the wealth tax have, at times, succeeded. Several regional attempts to reduce or rebate it have also proven successful. But every new setback (Covid 19) or perceived setback to the Spanish economy causes the government to want to scurry back to reinstitute it and/or reduce the limitations previously placed on it. At the end of the day, now that the wealth tax has been established, it's likely too big a temptation as a source of taxation income for the national government *not* to keep it around in some form. Thus, it's another shoe that has to be worn. It may get misplaced at those times when the Spanish national economy is doing well, but it will return.

Spain, together with Norway and Switzerland are the only European OECD countries currently with a wealth tax. France and Italy, for example, have wealth taxes on selected assets, but not on one's wealth.

All of which means that TAXES is a particularly uncomfortable, non-matching pair of shoes for any American living in Spain. The U.S. is the only major country that keeps citizens tethered to a tax leash even long after they've moved out of the country, while Spain is one of the handful of countries with a wealth tax.

Are there any other factors about TAXES to keep in mind? Yes, trusts are one. Spain has a legal system based on civil law which doesn't allow for the creation of trusts. The U.S. legal system is based on common law, so it does. Thus, an American reporting a trust and its income for her taxes in Spain can be expensive and complex. This applies both to those gifting assets to a U.S. trust as well as the trust's beneficiaries. Because trusts have different tax implications in Spain than in the States, they can significantly increase one's Spanish tax burden.

*Note: 401Ks and IRAs are another topic briefly worth mentioning. Neither 401Ks nor IRAs receive the same favorable tax treatment in Spain as they do in the U.S. because Spain doesn't treat them under the local pension-advantaged status as they would a Spanish tax-deferred product or pension. Nonetheless, Americans living in Spain can still contribute to an IRA in the U.S., but the tax advantages they receive will only apply to their U.S. taxes.*

When it comes to taxes, it's rare to run across an even moderately interesting topic. But I've discovered one: the IRS requires that tax returns be presented using U.S. dollars ($) as the currency. So, Americans working in Spain need an exchange rate to convert the euros they earn into dollars to file their U.S. 1040 tax return.

For dividends or other occasional payments, the IRS allows you to use the published exchange rate for that day. For salary or other periodic payments, there's an exchange rate for the year published by the IRS. I love that. If the IRS had a resumé, surely "collect U.S. taxes" would appear at the top, but I'm glad to know they could have an entry for OTHER or HOBBIES at the bottom: "publish annual exchange rates".

Can you imagine the amount of politicking and jostling that goes into deciding the IRS's euro/dollar exchange rate for an entire year? This might call for a new joke. Up until now, my favorite IRS joke had been:

*Q; What did the terrorists who hijacked an airplane full of IRS agents do?*

*A: They threatened to release one every hour if their demands weren't met.*

But that was before I learned that the IRS publishes exchange rates each year. Here's the type of joke I see lurking out there-

> *Q: How many IRS employees does it take to calculate the euro/ dollar exchange rate each year?*

As we've seen, TAXES don't fit Americans in Spain too well. Maybe the shoes in the box labeled INVESTMENTS are a better fit?

## INVESTMENTS

To try on the American INVESTMENTS shoe, one shoehorn is named PFIC. The first problem with PFIC is it doesn't have enough vowels to be pronounced easily. It stands for "Passive Foreign Investment Company". The second, and much bigger, problem is how costly and unfair it can seem to Americans living outside the U.S.

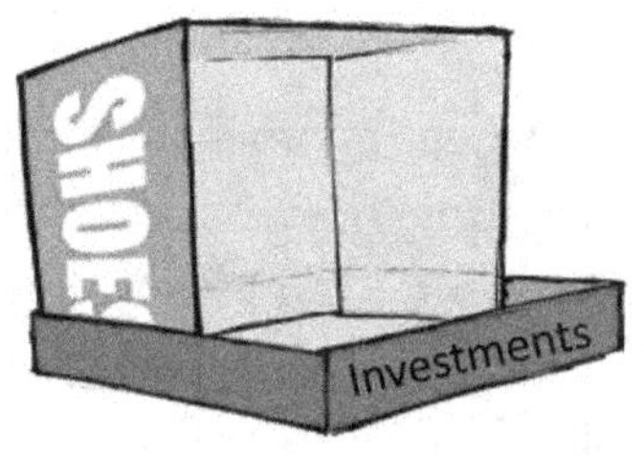


In theory, this IRS rule responds to a lack of clarity in holdings of some foreign accounts or businesses, by which overseas tax filers can delay the declaration of what would otherwise be current income (and therefore subject to taxes that year) by simply waiting until the asset in question is one-day sold and declaring it all as a capital gain.

And the IRS would be none the wiser because the differing language and/or accounting or reporting standards keep them from knowing what's really inside the account or business. So, the presumed assumption is "you're holding this asset or business for the purpose of not being transparent." Unfortunately, PFIC rules apply to both mutual funds and ETFs managed outside the United States, assets that *are* generally transparent.

So, on the one hand, a T. Rowe Price World Bond Fund managed in Baltimore, which invests exclusively outside the States would *not* be subject to PFIC rules. The idea is the IRS can see clearly what bonds T.

Rowe Price holds in this fund. On the other hand, a mutual fund that's managed in Spain, even if it were to hold U.S. treasury bonds, *is* subject.

PFIC rules penalize, both in terms of tax preparation time to detail lots of stuff, and in terms of a punitive tax rates, any "passive" investments outside the U.S.

Perhaps the folks at the IRS were influenced by an idea in criminology known as the "broken windows theory": that signs of anti-social behavior or crime create an environment that encourages further crime and disorder. According to the theory, policing methods that target minor crimes such as fare evasion, graffiti, and jaywalking help to create an atmosphere of order and lawfulness. The theory was popularized in the 1990's by New York City police commissioner William Bratton and mayor Rudy Gulliani, and is discussed by author Malcom Gladwell in his amazing book "The Tipping Point".

Maybe the IRS thought that Americans overseas, seeing a few dishonest taxpayers take advantage of the lack of transparency of foreign securities, might be tempted to imitate their actions. Maybe that's true. If so, I think the IRS fixed one "broken window" but knocked down the door in doing so.

Whatever their reasoning, PFIC rules make buying a Spanish mutual fund a less-than-perfect fit for Americans in Spain. Thankfully, assets such as individual stocks and real estate are not subject to PFIC rules.

So, you might be asking, if PFIC is a problem for *foreign* mutual funds or ETFs, why don't Americans in Spain simply buy *American* mutual funds or ETFs? They're Americans, after all. Unfortunately, it's here that MiFID II—one of the referees we saw when discussing Spain's investment management world—jumps onto the playing field.

I might have an overactive imagination, but this is the way I think things happened:

Imagine if you had an important job with the European Union a dozen or so years ago, and you saw the behemoth American mutual fund/ETF industry poised like a bully to eat the lunch of your skinny teenaged European mutual fund/EFT industry. How would you have responded? You want to help get your fledging young industry off the ground. But the inherent advantages and the head-start that the big American firms have in terms of size, expertise, track record and marketing prowess is enormous. You could cede your lunch to this big bully every day. Or you could find a creative way to banish the bully from your lunchroom entirely.

In my opinion the European Union discovered a way to implement the second method, displaying a good bit of creativity along the way. They fought off the bully while at the same time being able to claim credit for "safeguarding" individual investors. How? The EU's Markets in Financial Institutions II (MiFID II) established rules designed to "protect" small investors that require funds to disclose future performance under four scenarios. Sounds reasonable. However, U.S. legislation precludes American funds or ETFs from making such forecasts. Curiously, European funds *can* make such forecasts. Two birds with one stone, if you ask me: help protect the personal investor while simultaneously allowing your nascent local industry to grow by keeping a big foreign bully out of your lunchroom.

It's too clever to be labeled as protectionism. It's not a tariff or an embargo. But for Americans in Europe, it might feel like one. That's because these rules apply to anyone residing in Europe, it's not based on nationality.

Thus, Americans in Spain, just like those in the rest of Europe, are left with a difficult road to buy American mutual funds/ETFs because of MiFID II and a costly and difficult road to buy European mutual funds/ETFs because of PFIC.

So, that's two pairs of bad-fitting shoes, TAXES and INVESTMENTS. What about the third pair, FINANCIAL INSTITUTIONS?

# FINANCIAL INSTITUTIONS

The Foreign Account Tax Compliance Act (FATCA) is a 2010 U.S. tax law that requires foreign financial institutions to disclose the identities of U.S. citizens and the value of their assets held in their accounts to the IRS. FATCA strikes me as a funny name. But foreign financial 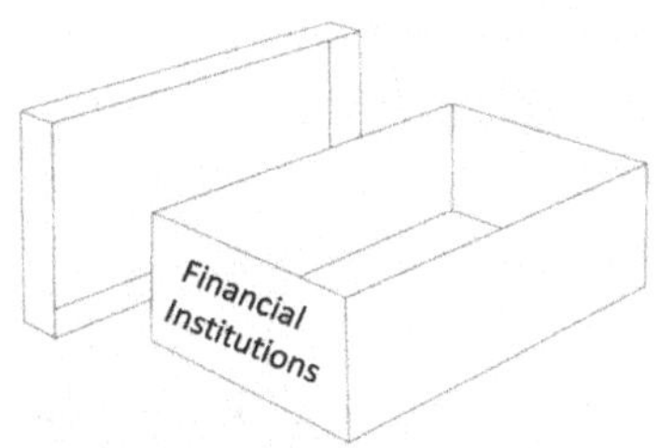

institutions that don't comply with it aren't laughing. They'll not only be excluded from the U.S. market but will also have 30% of the amount of any payment they're otherwise owed in the U.S. deducted and withheld from them as a tax penalty.

FATCA was intended to form the basis for a relationship between the U.S. Department of the Treasury and countries/financial institutions around the globe. It's a tax *enforcement* law, but it's not a tax. It was introduced as part of the Hiring Incentives to Restore Employment (HIRE) Act. One of the HIRE Act incentives offered to employers included an increase in business tax credit for each new employee hired. Funding the costs of these incentives, Congress included revenue-generating provisions in the HIRE Act through FATCA.

In 2021, the Global Compliance Institute certified me as a FATCA specialist, so I feel qualified to offer my unsolicited opinion. FATCA must have sounded like a good theory to swivel-chair bureaucrats in Washington D.C. one day: *"how can we collect more taxes from Americans overseas? Why don't we grab foreign financial institutions by their feet and hold them over a cliff, like in cartoons, and threaten to drop them if they don't provide us information about the accounts of their American clients?"*

But FATCA fails to follow a basic principle of international bilateral agreements: mutual benefit. There's neither benefit nor reciprocity for foreign financial institutions nor foreign governments if they comply with FATCA. Yet stiff penalties await them if they don't.

Whatever their thinking was, Washington clearly failed to predict that the reaction of many of these foreign financial institutions would be swift and decisive: stop accepting Americans as clients. *"Why"*, these institutions reasoned, *"should we cater to the whims of the U.S. Department of the Treasury, who might accidentally drop us on our head, or may invoke some new rule about U.S. citizens' accounts when they get around to it, when there's an alternative that requires <u>no</u> investment and even more importantly <u>no</u> risk on our part: simply not accept Americans as clients?"* An easy fix, in their mind, although it does carry with it an opportunity cost.

Thus, a great many Americans expats across the globe watched as their local financial institutions pulled the rug out from under them, just as many more won't accept them as new clients.

The estimated numbers are lopsided and bad.

On the cost side, the Swiss-American Chamber of Commerce Report estimated FATCA worldwide implementation costs of between $500 billion and $1 trillion, and that FATCA running costs would be $10–$30 billion globally.

Yet, on the revenue side, the United States Congress Joint Committee on Taxation estimated FATCA would produce an average of only $792 million in additional tax revenue a year. At that rate, it would take more than 630 years simply to recover the global costs of initially implementing it. Revenue projections from organizations other than the U.S. Congress were even lower.

To Americans living abroad, only a lack of functioning calculators in Washington could explain how an Act with such errant math could ever have been instituted. Their bigger problem is the difficulty in trying to open a simple bank or investment account, or in keeping your existing account open, simply because they're an American. Due to FATCA, being labeled a "U.S. Person" by a Spanish financial institution isn't too different than if one were in Salem, Massachusetts in the 1690's and accused of being a "witch". The biggest difference being that the trial by water test—to see if we'll sink or float—isn't necessary because in our case we've already been declared "guilty".

Does it matter that the theory formulated in Washington didn't fit well with reality? I'm typically an optimistic person, but in this case I don't think so. Unlike the "flat earth" theorist who decided to prove his theory by walking to the end of the world but in the end came around (*that*, by the way, is a joke), no one in Washington seems to be "coming around" on the topic of FATCA.

So, opening and maintaining a bank account in Spain is not easy for most. That's one FINANCIAL INSTITUTIONS shoe that doesn't fit well.

Fortunately, in many cases, a better fit is keeping their American accounts. If they still have one, that is. The U.S. Patriot Act, however, made maintaining/obtaining American accounts a bit more difficult.

In the aftermath of the September 11 terrorist acts which destroyed the World Trade Center Towers in New York in 2001, investigations began almost immediately into how to prevent a similar event from ever happening. Yet, despite untold time, effort and resources spent scrutinizing the matter, the experts were unable to find a surefire measure that could protect against a similar attack. However, investigations did reveal that the sums of money the terrorists spent for aviation school, travel, rent and other expenses in the U.S. *could* have been tracked in the months leading up to the attack.

Thus, when the U.S. Patriot Act was enacted to combat terrorism that same year, it introduced regulations requiring all banks to "Know Your Customer" ("KYC"). The Act *"requires all financial institutions to obtain, verify, and record information that identifies each person who opens an account or changes an existing account. This federal requirement applies to all new customers and current customers."*

The ramifications in Spain, which in 2004 in Madrid suffered its own deadly terrorist attacks at the hands of al-Qaeda, are that Americans face more scrutiny from their existing American banks or investment accounts if their Spanish address is listed on the account forms. As a result, they may have a more difficult time opening or maintaining an American account. Some Americans living overseas steer clear of this by providing the U.S. address of a trusted friend or family member to their U.S. financial institutions. This isn't foolproof, but it often works.

Because the topic has been shoeboxes, let's not look at a Venn diagram drawn with circles. Instead, let's look at a "Vans" diagram (borrowing for a moment the name of the California skateboarding shoe manufacturer) drawn with shoebox-shaped rectangles:

**VANS** diagram

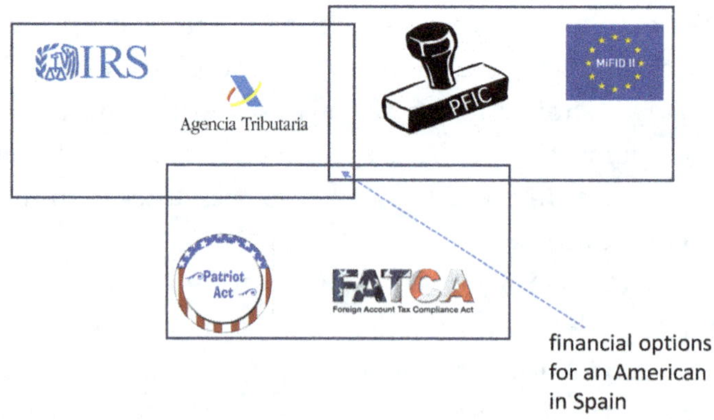

## WHERE DOES THIS LEAVE US?

As we've seen, no one-size-fits-all financial solution for Americans in Spain will work. As an American in Spain myself, I personally relate to these challenges. As a financial planner certified in Spain, I can help my fellow countrymen overcome them. And because I work for BISSAN Wealth Management, I can search for the perfect product or service based on the client's exact circumstances, not sales quotas.

# CHAPTER 10

# CONCLUSION

**IN CHAPTER 1, WE** began our journey in a leafy neighborhood in Valencia, Spain. In chapter 2, an astronaut explained a method of financial planning to us. In chapter 3, we convinced a skeptic of the value of financial planning. In chapter 4, we were introduced to the financial advisory referees, playing field, and players in Spain. In chapter 5, we learned how BISSAN Wealth Management checks all the boxes. In chapter 6, we saw risk management's importance, ratios, and a method of planning that prioritizes insurance. In chapter 7, we were introduced to the BISSAN method. In chapter 8, we learned about EFPA Spain's credentials. In chapter 9, we saw the circumstances that confront Americans in Spain re taxes, investments, and financial institutions.

Thanks to Columbus sailing on his voyages from Spain long ago, we learned that the idea that the Old World was the only world would need to be reexamined, and that maps would need to be redrawn.

Financial planning, I think, is the New World re-crossing the same ocean to return the favor. It's showing Spain that its old financial advisory model needs to be reexamined, and its policies may need to be redrawn.

At BISSAN Wealth Management we're working to ensure that this new map includes transparent, unbiased, objective financial planning assistance no matter what your net worth.

If you're an American in Spain, please feel free to contact me. If you're not, please pass this book along when you meet someone who is.

# A FEW STORIES

## I STILL DON'T KNOW WHY THERE WAS A MARCH IN THE FIRST PLACE (BUENOS AIRES, ARGENTINA)

**I'M STAYING SIX BLOCKS** from Argentina's National Congress—it's an imposing building. In its shadow, I witnessed a large march on Friday.

As an uninvited foreigner, I was overly conscious of my appearance and body language while watching the march. Not wanting to appear oppositional, I took care to not frown, cross my arms or looks skeptical. At the same time, I didn't want to appear too supportive, somehow swept up in the arms of a group and spontaneously voted into blood-oath membership of a political affiliation of which I've never heard.

My acute self-awareness was completely unwarranted. No one paid me the slightest bit of attention. In fact, nobody paid attention to anyone but themselves. It was a self-expressive gathering of marchers, it seemed.

I should provide a disclaimer here: I've never taken a formal "Sign-reading in Spanish" class. As a result, I may be somehow confusing names or slogans of some groups. Socialist, Anarchist (not an easy group of marchers to organize, I don't imagine) and Green parties were easy to identify.

Other groups, like Skateboarding Ruined My Life and Mothers Against Inflation seemed less so. Some I could only venture a guess at- Pizza Delivery Separatists (they won't deliver combo pizzas?) and

Hospital Surgeon Revolutionaries (revolt against the food served in the hospital cafeteria?) are two examples. And certain combination groups weren't intuitive affiliations: Grape Pickers, Taxi Drivers and Mattress Owners Unite was one. Some were downright contradictory: Party of Multi-National Grassroots Nationalistic Regionalists.

In addition to the wide range of groups, there were a range of marching strategies – most waved banners, many pumped fists or chanted slogans, others played drums, and some had a truck replete with speakers to drive in front of their marchers as a microphoned singer led the group in song—or sang solo in the case of complicated group anthems.

On one of these trucks, the unfortunate woman singer had a corded microphone but wanted to walk in solidarity with her fellow marchers rather than ride in the truck. She was spirited, wanting to face her brethren group members to exhort them in song. This meant she walked backwards, with her back to the truck. I heard a thud. She'd crashed into the rear of the truck when it stopped suddenly. Whenever her truck sped up again, she needed to scurry to catch it before it yanked her microphone from her. At times, these miscalculations adversely impacted her singing efforts. But never her spirit.

Equal parts high school marching band rehearsal, small-town USA 4th of July parade and Baptist Church revival, this event had none of the gallantry of Macy's parade floats. Some marchers carried what looked like yard sale items. One marched the wrong direction. One group even passed another, not ideologically, but probably because the group ahead was walking too slow.

Yet, the disorganized, at-times-perplexing event sometimes had me tapping my foot. Or getting goose bumps. Or feeling sad. Or cheering. Or feeling inexplicably proud. Or wanting to sing. Or wanting to march. Or all those things at once.

I don't know why there was a march, but never in life did NBC's live telecast of the Thanksgiving Day Parade, hosted by some overly dramatic television celebrity, make me feel any of that.

# EL SALVADOR

**IT'S A HUMID NIGHT,** picnic tables arranged throughout a small courtyard. At our table I sit with two other Americans and three Salvadorans. As our conversation ricochets from politics to soccer to law, I realize I haven't touched a bite of food. I momentarily wonder why. But thirty seconds later I'm swept up in a new discussion on El Salvadoran education and forget my food altogether again. By the end of the evening, I've eaten maybe six bites.

Jenny Craig or Weight Watchers may want to patent my new discovery: you can't eat if the Americans at your table don't speak Spanish and the Spanish-speakers don't speak a word of English; however, everyone wants to communicate. I needed to listen to and then translate every question and every answer. It's not that talking burns a significant number of calories, it's that all the talking left me no time to eat. No diet plan could be more effective. Jenny Craig may want to change its motto *"we're about moderation"* to *"moderation through conversation."* And Weight Watchers may want to borrow my idea, maybe with a slogan such as: *"Try Translating instead of Trans-fatting"*.

But it's worth it. The Americans are a delightful couple who sponsor two children at this home for orphans and ask questions that are consistently thoughtful and tough to translate. One of the Salvadorans is the director of this home for orphans and two are its inhabitants. Of the two, I've forgotten the name of the other orphan, but I remember Telma (think "Thelma" but a Spanish version).

Oh, sorry, some background might be helpful: I'm here in El Salvador visiting my third home for orphans of NPH (*Nuestros Pequeños Hermanos)* or "Our little brothers and sisters", in English. Our American group is here to participate in the celebration of the home's recent high school graduates. If you've ever once been excited at an American high school graduation, imagine the pride of getting your diploma despite having been orphaned or abandoned as a child, and living in a country as poor and marginalized as El Salvador. These kids are the underdogs of underdogs.

Many of the Americans traveling here sponsor one of the graduating children. Or maybe one of their siblings. It's an exciting time, made even more so by the arrival of our group of Americans and the great way the home has of including and acknowledging everyone involved.

The day before, just after the graduation ceremony, I made sure to personally congratulate and shake the hand of each and every one of the 19 graduates as they were lined up awaiting a photo session. All were polite. But because I had never met any of them before, some were a bit confused, thinking maybe I had mistaken them for someone else.

At dinner in the courtyard, seating arrangements are random. The food arrives late. And once it does, we all sit in groups of six at the nearest table to where we'd happen to be standing.

I ask Telma and her friend the usual questions during dinner. When I ask what year of school she's in, Telma seems surprised. She's one of the students whose hand I'd shaken the day before, one of the high school grads. To me, being one of 265 children here and not still wearing her cap & gown of the day before are valid excuses for not remembering her. To her, a stranger that would take the time to shake her hand and congratulate her means a lot.

You see, Telma isn't one of the pretty girls her age and she's quite likely the shyest. The director of the orphanage is a kind man—my guess is he was talking to her and her friend when we all sat to eat because he looks out for the underdogs of the group. Telma's shyness is so extreme that when she talks it's in a rush to get words out and she delivers them in a nearly undecipherable heap. She then gets embarrassed, withdraws again, and it's a long wait before her next mad dash of unintelligible words. I would never have gotten the opportunity to know her if it weren't for being randomly seated in the same small group together.

I already sponsor a 13-year-old in the NPH home in Guatemala. Luis, whose mother died two years ago, is a great little guy that NPH assigned to me. I wasn't looking for another, yet I don't think I have a choice but to sponsor Telma. So, for movie fans, I'll soon be "godparent" to two Central American children: Telma and Luis.

There are some decisions we make in our life, I think, where we're not really the one in the driver's seat. My decision to sponsor Telma is one of those. Although I've now met hundreds of kids at three Central American homes for orphans, she's the one I know I should sponsor. In a marginalized country like El Salvador, a shy and socially awkward teenage orphan will face many challenges in life. But she now has a new American sponsor to lend a hand.

## LOUDSPEAKER THAT'S NOT LOUD (LIMA, PERU)

**LOUDSPEAKER ANNOUNCEMENT** in the Lima airport-

*"Ladies and Gentlemen, we're set for takeoff so would the following passengers please do their best to maybe hurry up just a bit to the gate if you can: the Rodriguez family, Mr. Medina, the Romero family, Dr. Suarez, the Diaz family....Oh, look who's here! The Romero family is at the gate! Hello, Mrs. Romero, that's a lovely dress. Well, okay, that means we're now only missing these passengers. the Rodriguez family, Mr. Medina,...One moment, Mr. Romero, do you happen to have your son's boarding pass? Yes, I can hold your coffee while you look for it....Sorry,....we now ask the following passengers to maybe speed up a small bit their pace toward the gate, if they don't mind, starting with the Rodriguez family, Mr. Medina, Dr. Suarez..."*

## COFFEE IN NICARAGUA

**THERE IS NO STARBUCKS** in Granada, Nicaragua. I'm happy about that. Don't get me wrong, I enjoy Starbucks. But it's somehow reassuring that the world is not *one place*, that there are still differences between distinct parts of the world.

We do have local coffee shops that are Starbucks knockoffs here. The hotel I'm staying in serves such bad coffee that I've been forced to try these. Casa de Café is one. Their coffee is also bad. At least my hotel has an excuse — guest service is their core competence, not coffee.

Just as they do in the hotel, these coffee shops serve their coffee scaldingly hot. The trick here, I now believe, is to drink your coffee at just the right moment. You need to let it cool sufficiently to prevent third degree burns but not so much that you can *taste* the coffee.

There's no method to cool down the coffee in Nicaragua, you see, except waiting. There's no milk or cream here. Say goodbye to soy or almond milk or lactose intolerant choices altogether. Even in these coffee shops. Their condiment stands have only sugar, napkins and those cup sleeves — which don't help in combating the blazing hot temperatures at which they serve Nicaraguan coffee, even if you were to wrap it in a dozen insulating sleeves.

It seems ironic that Nicaragua, where the combination of climate and soil produces such rich coffee beans, does not have a *coffee culture*. Young mothers don't meet at Casa de Café to complain about their kids' nannies. That's for folks in wealthy countries.

Drinking hot beverages isn't in accord with temperatures here. Cold drinks, now *that* is the answer to combat Nicaraguan heat. Nor is caffeine particularly helpful in this climate. The Spanish language school I'm attending here has a coffee maker that produces coffee just as bad as the hotel coffee. When the afternoon heat hits, it doesn't matter how much of it I've drunk, I don't have the energy to do anything. Caffeine is powerless to change this.

The problem may have its origin in colonial times. As a de-facto American colony, Nicaragua's best products historically have been exported abroad. The only way to obtain good coffee back then was to import it. The stuff served domestically would have been poor quality.

How little has changed.

I ask Ramon, my favorite employee at the hotel: "Do you think there will be a Starbucks in Granada one day in the future?

Ramon: "*What's Stray box*?!?"

## A WILD RIDE

**THERE IS NO DIRECT** Guatemala to Chicago flight, so we flew to Miami first. But I only noticed 3 others on the plane to Chicago: a five-year old boy sitting with his dad, the flight's captain, and the slowest-moving flight attendant in the history of airline travel.

Captain Doublespeak (known to friends as 'Captain Double talk') squawks over our PA: "welcome aboard, we apologize for the delays and we'll try to make it up to you while we're in the air by flying faster but because, of course, we really can't do that, we won't."

5-year-old: "Dad, will they give us apple sauce? Dad am I in my seat?! Dad, are we in Chicago?"

Captain Doublespeak over PA: "I enjoy giving passengers the freedom to move about the cabin as much as possible. Of course, I'll keep the Fasten Seat Belt sign, indicating that you need to return to your seat, illuminated our entire flight "

5-year-old: "Dad, what if the plane runs out of gas? Dad, is your Seat Belt Sign on? Can I have a piece of pie with ice cream? Dad, what if I have to sneeze while the plane is on?"

Slow-moving Flight Attendant tentatively steers beverage cart into aisle after looking both ways as if she's trying to merge onto high-speed highway traffic.

Captain Doublespeak: "we'll be encountering some very rough air. I'll do my best to avoid it and I know that won't work so instead I'll drive us right into it and I know that's a bad idea so I want to thank you for flying with us tonight, we know you have a choice in airlines..."

5-year-old: "dad, can I stay up past my bedtime? Dad, are we in the air yet?! Dad, do they have a swing set on the plane?"

After nearly twelve minutes maneuvering her cart, Flight Attendant Molasses asks a passenger what they'd like to drink. She methodically lists every beverage available.

5-year-old: "Dad, can I fall asleep on the airplane? Dad, what if someone gets on the plane and then has a Birthday?!"

Flight Attendant Molasses: "...and we serve all Coke products, sprite, ginger ale, apple juice, tomato juice, cranberry juice, coffee, tea, water, Sierra mist, club soda..." She has yet to give anyone in the first row a beverage.

5-year-old: "dad, what if the plane breaks? Dad, can we play hide-and-seek on the plane?"

Passenger to Flight Attendant Molasses: "I'd like tomato juice, please"

Attendant Molasses: "wouldn't you like to know all your choices first? we serve all Coke products, sprite, ginger ale,..."

Passenger: "no, I think I'd just like tomato juice"

Attendant Molasses: "...oh, and we also have alcohol for purchase..."

Passenger: "no, just tomato juice!"

Attendant Molasses: "would you like ice with that?"

Captain Doublespeak: "We have a lot of sophisticated navigational technology at our disposal here in the cockpit. Of course, for your safety and comfort, I'm not using any of it..."

With a pair of tongs, Attendant Molasses purposefully drops one ice cube at a time into a cup. She waits for each ice cube to hit bottom before reaching for the next. A diamond cutter wouldn't have moved as delicately.

5-year-old: "dad, do you know where my other shoe is? Dad, can we have a sing-along? Dad are we in row 29?"

Attendant Molasses starts reciting the list of beverage choices to the next person. Her cart remains rooted to the same spot in the aisle.

Captain Doublespeak: "there's a great view of the mighty Mississippi River off the right side of our plane. Unfortunately, it's way too dark to see anything at this hour."

Impatient passengers are simply grabbing stuff off Attendant Molasses's cart by now. She readies herself to serve passengers in the second row.

# OUTSIDE A SMALL NICARAGUAN TOWN

**MOVE ASIDE, PEACE CORPS.** Pack your bags, Red Cross. Post your resumé on social media, United Nations, and update your Facebook profile while you're at it. Why? Six teenage American girls who just visited the "Nuestros Pequeños Hermanos" (NPH) orphanage in Nicaragua contributed more to international relations than all your symposiums and experts do.

Outwardly, these girls appear incapable of outshining massive international relief organizations. They look like everyday midwestern American teens because that's what they are. But don't be fooled; there's a special sauce to their recipe. It's simple really: they offered kindness and compassion to every one of the dozens of abandoned & orphaned Nicaraguan kids they encountered at the NPH home. Nothing less. Nothing more. Believe me, their recipe works.

How they jointly came upon this recipe is a mystery. Most of the girls had little connection to each other before the trip: they're from two American cities, various high schools. Yet they got along well. Sure, a wet towel was left atop another's bed in the room they shared. And some conversations ended abruptly when the response "OBVI" was an answer to one girl's question. ('OBVI' is short for "Obviously"—implying that the respondent can't be bothered to even articulate a full word answer of ridicule to the question).

But getting along with each other was not the remarkable trait of these six teenagers—how they reached out to the Nicaraguan kids was.

An all-time favorite story of mine is a Taoist tale that appears in *"Raise High the Roof Beam, Carpenters"*, a book by J.D. Salinger.

In it, the duke of some kingdom long ago asks his aging trusted advisor how he should select his new horse. His counselor suggests the help of a younger man, but not his own son. He says that finding a superlative horse – one that raises no dust and leaves no tracks – is nearly impossible. That his own son lacks this elusive skill.

The young man suggested by the duke's counselor finds the duke a new horse. But, although the young man described it as a dun-colored mare, it was in fact a coal-black stallion. The duke wasn't pleased and complained to his counselor. His advisor is instead impressed upon hearing this, realizing that in making sure of the most essential characteristics of the horse, the young man had ignored the horse's details.

When the horse arrived, it turned out to be a truly superlative animal.

These teenage girls saw neither dun-colored mares nor Nicaraguans nor black stallions nor orphans. Like the young man in Salinger's Taoist tale, they saw inward; they saw fellow kids who need their love and compassion. And I think most days that's worth ten thousand of any us put together.


## SUNDAYS, LIKE CLOCKWORK (BUENOS AIRES, ARGENTINA)

TODAY IS SUNDAY, so I made sure to return to the clothes launderer I discovered last Sunday. It's the only day Diego works there.

*"You are Australian or American, I can ree-cognize from your face"* begins Diego in his unique English before I can inquire if this, in fact, is a launderer or if I'm mistakenly hoping to get my clothes cleaned by a barber shop.

His wife teaches English. So, he grabs any opportunity he can to practice speaking it. And I do mean grab. With both hands. Although we were straining our necks to talk through the small opening of a gate he'd shut just prior to my arrival, he continued: *"Do you know I sell gee-tars?"* as his hands rapidly pantomime the guitar-strumming motion, *"...do-ring the week? Theze I do for my o-coo-pation, to make my leeving. Hand-made gee-tars only, I must tell you!"*

Either I conveyed skepticism, or he couldn't see me well in the limited gate opening through which we were attempting to speak. So, he pulled his sleeve up to proffer evidence – a large guitar tattoo on his forearm. "In the states we have ID swipe badges," I wanted to inform him, "more efficient should you ever decide to switch careers."

I didn't say that. I didn't say much. And I didn't need to, he carried on quite well speaking for both of us. Do you know how his guitar company selects the one-in-a-thousand Oregon tree capable of becoming part of their custom guitars? I now do. Thankfully, they never invite Diego on these forest excursions; he'd still be there happily talking to the trees in English if they had.

Should I have interrupted to tell him that I simply wanted to drop off my laundry? I couldn't. He was too entertaining. And every time he made a motion toward writing up my laundry ticket, he'd then quickly distract himself with another tale. What Keith Richards honestly thinks of Mick Jagger's knighthood. Why touring with a musical group is tough on a marriage.

He likes speaking English. He claims he's learned much of it by reading the written lyrics of band's songs. It's not that I didn't TRY to add Spanish to our discussion. I volunteered an: *"I understand"* one time.

*"Yes"*—he acknowledged in English with a rapid and subtly dismissive nod, *"you speak words of the Spaneesh, no?"* – before delightedly steam-rolling on once again.

I even attempted to tell him in Spanish that I put the wet towel in a separate bag. He looked at me blankly. I tried again: *"MOJADA (wet) is the right word, isn't it?"* I asked, momentarily doubting myself. *"Oh yes,"* he replied rapidly in English, *"but you see that I will soon make everything MOJADA. So we have no worries about theze."*

His English, while accented, is good. His knowledge of music is exhaustive. His ability to entertain is off the charts. His ability to clean laundry, I'm still unsure of. What I am sure of is that next Sunday, like clockwork, I'll return. I wouldn't miss it.

When I return the following Sunday, Iron Maiden music nearly shakes the small windows of the laundromat. I smile without meaning to. Diego must be there.

*"You have low-cated me,"* he says grinning once he peaks his head out from the adjacent room. Initially getting his attention over the noise of active washers and dryers and blasting Iron Maiden music had been no easy task.

*"I was unable to hear, you must understand,"* he says in his one-of-a-kind English, *"because such loud music is playing. But in my heart I have such fondness for Iron Maiden, you see...,"* reaching to turn down the music as he speaks, *"always those drums – boom! Boom! Is a more powair-full sound aveel-able to us anywhere but in music, I must ask you?"*

I am glad to see him, I realize. Just being here again makes me happy.

He catapults his English into a rich discussion of Ozzy Osborne, once of Black Sabbath. How Ozzy is puzzled he remains alive after years of drug abuse. How Diego is puzzled Ozzy remains alive after years of drug abuse. *"Have you given thought to his lee-rics?"* he asks me. No, I think to myself, but the old television show featuring him and his cuckoo family in their house was sometimes funny.

*"His lee-rics are quite seemply, mind-blowing,"* he says, as he turns the music volume back up. His cadence in English is quickly gaining its legs and he now wants musical accompaniment for it: *"'you have eentro-duced me to my mind, Sweet Leaf,' for example, are words to his song of the same name. I am completely intreegued by these words. What can they mean? I ask of myself."*

Ozzy Osborne, he says, understandably baffled that he finds himself still alive after having abused drugs for so long, will donate his body to medical research when he dies. It surprises me that Diego is not thinking of doing the same.

Instead, he continues talking, *"...but Iron Maiden is just one of many bands that are for me, quite fascin-ayting,"* he announces.

He starts to play a ZZ Top song. *"ZZ top...,"* I explain to him in English, *"was the last concert I ever attended in the States. One of the two bearded musicians explained to the audience that day that they adhere to two strict rules at all concerts:*

1. *No drinking when they play Gospel songs*
2. *Don't play any Gospel songs"*

Diego nods at me approvingly. He likes this. This guy may just make it in this world after all, he appears to conclude about me.

He deviates from the topic of music only once: when we discuss my laundry ticket. We are both embarrassed, I realize, that such mundane trivia needs to be administered to amidst such a rich cultural exchange.

Yet if I weren't swept up in the parallel universe of another visit to the laundromat of Diego, I'd realize that getting my laundry washed is the purpose of my visit.

Or is it?

## EVEN 4 YEAR-OLD NORTH AMERICANS (SANTIAGO, CHILE)

**"*YOU'RE NORTH AMERICAN!*"** accuses the taxi driver as I enter his car, before I could so much as announce a destination. How did he know, I hadn't said a word? Aside from my mixed emotion at being unceremoniously lumped together with Canadians, I was intrigued.

Like Sherlock Holmes revealing his deductive reasoning to Dr. Watson, the cabbie explained that I had slammed the car door after entering. Even a 4-year-old North American (there's that word again) shut car doors too hard. And people from other continents don't slam car doors, he claims.

I think it's learned behavior. We often have bigger cars (or snowplows, if we're including Canadians) so we become accustomed to using more torque shutting doors. In my personal case, I received car door slamming training while living in New York City. Door slamming is the agreed-upon signal to a NYC cabbie that passengers are in and he's free to peel away recklessly from the curve at high speeds.

As I entered a different cab at the end of the evening, I made sure to shut the car door very gently, to avoid being immediately branded as a North American. *"I don't think your car door shut all the way,"* the cab driver barked at me, *"can you give it another try?"* At least that's what I think he said (it's so tough to know when everything is being said in Spanish)

## CABBIE (BUENOS AIRES, ARGENTINA)

**JUMPED IN THE BACK** of a cab Tuesday night. We start on our way. We talk. The taxi driver is intrigued that I'm taking Spanish classes here in Argentina. He wants to be a teacher. To demonstrate, he holds up a cab driver training manual. He wants to train fellow taxi drivers to score well on the exam. He admits he hasn't passed the exam yet himself, but he expects to soon. And I wonder: "first decide to TEACH the course, then see if you can PASS it? And if he hasn't passed, how is he allowed to drive a cab? Or is he?"

These are questions I didn't want to ask as he rockets us through the erratic traffic chaos of Buenos Aires. When he discovers I'll also study in Peru, he starts mocking how Peruvians talk. I start laughing. He starts laughing. Waving his arms in imitation, he's all the while miraculously avoiding collisions with buses, or pedestrians or cars. He's a gifted mimic. He's an even better driver.

Defensive driving entails being offensive here in Buenos Aires. Ironic but true. When 80% of drivers are actively cutting off other vehicles in the most abrupt ways possible, you're only dangerous if you're not doing so. He wasn't dangerous. But he was funny. He asked what I'd learned that day in Spanish class. Then he asked me why they were teaching me THAT.

*"How would I know?"* I respond.

*"How would you know?"* he repeats, as he narrowly avoids running into a bicyclist.

## *"I WANT TO PUT A DING IN THE UNIVERSE."* STEVE JOBS (TEGUCIGALPA, HONDURAS)

Inside a 3-room building at the Nuestros Pequeños Hermanos (NPH) ranch for orphaned and abandoned children in Tegucigalpa, Honduras

**"THIS IS STALE AIR,"** I think to myself as we enter the doorway. I'm next aware, after walking in, of the confused scattering of the room's inhabitants: a lone young woman on a couch, a girl in a wheelchair near her, a young woman standing against one wall apart from two others in wheelchairs. No one faces the same direction. No one converses.

A television plays in the corner. No one watches.

I'm accompanying Dan, an American volunteer and part of our group. He's asked me to join him as he spends time at the home for young ladies with impairments and disabilities (i.e., "special needs").

I silently but immediately regret my decision to join him. Being here makes me uncomfortable. No one offers us a place to sit. No one welcomes us. The air doesn't circulate. We don't know where to stand and we're both having great difficulty simply striking up a conversation. Any conversation.

I don't kid myself that Dan invited me along for my charm alone; I'm here in part to help translate. But, despite our efforts there's no conversation. One woman physically turns her back to us. Another explains that Carmen, the back-turner, is simply mad at the world and we shouldn't take it personally. We don't know if this explanation comes from a young lady with special needs or an NPH caregiver because no one has introduced themselves.

Our hope of parlaying this nugget of information about Carmen into a dialogue dies out immediately. No conversation ensues. We're at a loss. Even a basic conversation starter such as, "do you like playing soccer?" isn't relevant to these young ladies.

My discomfort grows. I look up at the minute hand of the clock which has stopped dead in its tracks. The stale air grows somehow staler to me.

Dan gets an idea. *"Can you explain to someone that I'm hoping to get a pencil and paper?"* he asks me. I translate. A search begins. One young lady returns from the other room with a range of items bearing no discernible similarity to pencil and paper. We offer her exaggerated thanks but continue to search. A pencil is found.

He draws a quick sketch of the face of the first girl able to bring him paper. She tilts her head and looks at it. She looks back at Dan's face and then back at his drawing.

He repeats the process for a second young lady. A third looks at his first drawing and immediately identifies Maria, the apparent name of the sketch's model. *"Maria!"*, she says loudly while pointing at her. Others in the room look up.

*"Draw me next!"* one of them says. *"No, draw me first!"* says another.

Dan sketches nearly all of them before the end of the evening, when we need to leave because it's "lights out" time at the home.

No one would claim his sketches are works of art. Certainly not Dan. The vast majority are recognizably his model's face, but not all. As demand for his work grew and became a clamor, he had to draw fast in a less than ideal setting.

However, you can't judge the impact of art by objective standards alone. His sketches made these girls happy. Or in some cases, disappointed that his reflection of how they look to the outside world isn't a pretty picture. But it made them feel alive. Noticed. Something about how he really looked at each of them, into their eyes, so that he could sketch them, awakened a type of human contact many of them seldom receive, I think.

*"Daniel"* one of the girls says suddenly as we depart. At that one moment, everything seems so perfectly right in the world.

Personal space is cherished at an orphanage. The locker of each girl in the home is the one place they can preserve what is personally important to them- photos of family members, meaningful mementos. After our visit I was told that only one of the girls he sketched doesn't keep his drawing proudly displayed in their personal locker. She carries it around in her wheelchair with her.

I think Dan "put a ding in the universe" that night. If you listened closely, you may have heard it.


## IGUAZU FALLS, ARGENTINA

**AFTER NAVIGATING OUR WAY** down wet and steeply meandering steps, our 12-member group arrives at the boat launch. We're standing at a dock in Iguazu National Park, poised to be taken by boat into the mist of Iguazu's famous waterfalls. We're ready.

How did I get here? I ask myself.

Several sources had advised me to visit. Like Victoria Falls in Africa and Niagara Falls on the US/Canadian border, Iguazu Falls on the Paraguay/Argentina/Brazil border can also boast of being the "biggest" falls. One of these 3 waterfalls has the most water, another the steepest fall or the most waster falling per second or the widest falls area…Well, you get the picture. After visiting any of the three, you can tell your friends you've seen the world's "biggest" waterfall by at least one important measure.

Iguazu's waterfalls themselves are within an Argentine national park. An army base is located next to it. The alleged need for a military post is that Iguazu borders two foreign countries. My suspicion is that the waterfalls are gorgeous, so why wouldn't the army want to pitch a permanent tent there?

I'd booked this trip at a Buenos Aires travel agency what now seems like a lifetime ago. It was only four days. The travel agency's bureaucratic system took forever.

Like other places in Argentina, there were useless stamps needed on meaningless forms at the travel agency. But where the travel agency demonstrates its bureaucratic brilliance is by also requiring SIGNATURES. Many of them. On nearly all their unnecessary forms. By the time we'd finished, I was on a first name basis with the travel agency's nighttime cleaning staff. My two-day itinerary could not have been simpler. We weren't planning a foreign invasion from Iguazu's army base, after all, just one quick trip within Argentina.

I land at Iguazu Airport to find my shuttle driver waiting. He says he's had this job for ten years. I venture a guess from his accent that he's Mexican. He's not. In fact, it's the first time anyone's said that in his ten years on the job. I make a mental note to stop trying to guess where people are from.

His nickname is Elvis, he explains expectantly, waiting for me to ask how on earth an Argentine would've come by such a nickname. Instead, I ask where the bathroom is. When I return, I see he's collected three other shuttle passengers: a Colombian gal named Carolina and a south African couple.

Carolina asks Elvis where she can find a dance club in town and we leave the airport.

We drop the South Africans off at their hotel. It's a Sheraton and it's beautiful, gleaming, and offers panoramic views of the falls because it's located within the park. I'd spent hours and hours within that travel agency, and even once did it occur to anyone to mention that there's this gorgeous hotel INSIDE Iguazu Park? Apparently not.

Carolina asks a Sheraton employee if they have a dance club. We drive off.

My hotel, the last stop, is rustic. Its only discernible perk is having thin plastic packets of both shampoo and conditioner. But as I lamentably discover while showering the next morning, with soap in my eyes and suds on my hands, the manufacturer of these plastic packets didn't even pretend there's a perforated area or red tab from which you can open their products.

I'll go out on a limb and predict that this shampoo and conditioner manufacturer's impregnable plastic packet has never once accidentally opened or spilled during transport or storage. Ever opened at all, in fact.

"Oh, *you speak a bit of Spanish, good, here's the bus for you,*" says Carlos the guide as he directs me to a big tour bus later that morning.

"*Welcome aboard,*" announces Carlos on his bus microphone as the bus starts moving. "*Today we have multiple passengers from Argentina, Colombia, Chile and even one American!*" That must be me, I reason.

We arrive at the park and introduce ourselves. Nearly everyone on that bus at some point during the day came up and chatted with me. Nearly everyone on that bus, I learned, has a sister or brother or uncle or aunt or friend or cousin who lives or lived in Miami. Their warmth would have made it a great day even if we weren't in a stunning park.

Of course, I already knew Carolina from the shuttle bus the day before. She introduced her friends to me and asked if my hotel had a dance club.

My Spanish is now sufficient to be asked aboard a tour bus of native Spanish speakers. That doesn't mean I understand every word. Curiously, sometimes my comprehension kicks in only after a conversation has ended:

An Argentine had introduced himself and he and I were standing close to the bottom of the Iguazu waterfall. "Do you know this water originates in Brazil?!" he shouts, scarcely audible above the deafening cascade of water in front of us. "No, I'm from the United States originally!" I mistakenly yell to him in response. He seems unsure where he can take our conversation from there. Only later do I realize my mistake, too late to set the record straight for him.

# A FINAL NOTE

**GET ASKED OCCASIONALLY IF** I miss working on Wall Street. My answer surprises even me because I reminisce about something I didn't always enjoy at the time: my interactions with the bond "desk".

Investment banks have a peculiarity that many types of businesses don't: not only do they primarily have just two categories of customers, but the two groups seldom agree with each other. One group is the sellers, the companies or entities or governments issuing bonds or stocks or selling other assets. Across the table from them are the buyers, the companies or individuals or groups who, with the right price and conditions, might want to buy or lease these assets.

And investment banks have both as clients. At the same time. Think about what a delicate balancing act this needs to be.

If you were in the market to buy a house, you wouldn't hire the real estate agent who'd sold the seller's last two homes and is selling this one as *your* agent, to negotiate for you.

So how do investment banks do it?

Wall Street has convinced the world there's an effective "Chinese Wall" (not my term, it's the industry term as it makes reference to the historic and impenetrable Great Wall of China): a virtual barrier which, in an effort to avoid conflicts of interest, separates departments and *blocks* undesired exchanges of information between groups within the bank.

It's as if only information that somehow helps both sides can get through. But how is that possible? It's curious when you stop and think about it, isn't it?

The result is that bond departments of investment banks typically have an "origination" group: "bankers" working with entities that might want to issue bonds in the market. Across the wall from them sits the "sales and trading" group. These are the folks involved in the buying and selling of said bonds. They're the ones with whom I miss interacting. They're not called bankers, instead they're "traders" or "salespeople". Some financial institutions have an emphasis on one side or the other of this separation, but virtually all have some version of the two camps: origination bankers and sales/trading desks.

Sales and trading members often work on a *desk* so that information is more easily passed between themselves. They perform their job from an open floor lacking barriers which might otherwise separate them from their colleagues nearby. It's referred to as the desk. If you cherish your privacy, the desk would not be a good place for you. In front of each salesperson or trader sit the terminals and phones and other devices connecting them to their markets, news outlets, customers—different depending on what they sell or trade.

Salespeople are the most direct corollary to what the bankers originating the bonds do. Their customers are the insurance companies or bond funds or individuals who might buy said bonds when they're first issued. Many of the activities that occur after that are the domain of the traders: buying/selling of bonds after they've sold the new bonds to whoever first purchased them. Also on the sales desk is a "syndications" group, folks who coordinate with other banks when more than one bank is involved in a bond sale.

Let's use Ford Motor Company as an analogy. It doesn't fit precisely, but if it helps give us a mental picture, great. If not, I'm sure Ford Motor Company will understand and try to move on.

**Bankers** - it's their job to ensure that new cars roll off the factory floor with some frequency, that there's a perpetual supply of shiny new cars.

**Salespeople** - work for the car dealership. Maybe not in all cases, perhaps they specialize in selling fleets of cars directly from the factory to rental car agencies. But in general, they're the ones selling the new cars just after they've rolled off the Ford factory floor. The good ones may even have been involved in getting a car custom-made in the factory based on their client's specifications. Many of them, though, are content selling whatever model, style or color is rolling off the factory floor.

- **Sales syndication** – if Ford has a joint venture with another car manufacturer, they would exchange and coordinate information with the joint venture partner regarding any sales that involve cars from both manufacturers.

**Traders** - while some might do business inside the dealership, or maybe even the factory, traders typically buy and sell used cars, either from car wholesalers or from used car lots or even individuals.

So, we've got two sides: 1) bankers and 2) sales & trading. Each side represents a different client. Clients, in fact, that have diametrically opposed goals and desires.:

- A banker's client wants to sell her bonds at the lowest interest rate she can reasonably obtain, while encumbering herself with as few obligations as possible.
- A salesman's client wants the bond he buys to offer the highest interest rate while being protected fully from future events that could possibly preclude this.

The working conditions of these two sides aren't too similar, either. The hours of sales & trading are generally strict: when their market is open, they're generally needed at their desk. Banker hours, aside from obligations necessitated by events like roadshows or presentations, are often more flexible. But there's a price to be paid for the more flexible hours of a banker, that their workday is often longer. There's almost always more that can be done on the banking side, so a distinction between nights and weekends and sometimes even holidays can be blurred.

On the other hand, when the market for a sales/trading employee is *not* open—weekends, nights (except in cases such as that of a NYC trader who trades Japanese bonds), holidays – the need for them to be there is relaxed or even unnecessary. Client entertainment such as shows/dinners is a big exception to this, but we're talking in broad generalities here.

Senior bankers frequently travel. There's a cost to not spending time with clients and prospective clients. Senior sales and trading folks are frequently at their desk. There's a cost to be paid from being out of touch with what's happening in the market at that moment.

So, what does this former banker miss most about the bond desk? That sales and trading folks are the biggest collection of childish-acting adults you'll ever find. Or maybe the biggest collection of children having adult jobs, I don't know which.

What do I mean by that?

Sales and traders are more influenced by peer pressure, have shorter attention spans and have a straighter-to-the-point bluntness than other adults running around in this world. Maybe it's because folks on the desk sit about the same distance from each other as kids in a kindergarten class, I don't know.

## SHORT ATTENTION SPAN

When it's on their screen, their focus can often be laser-like. When it's not, forget about it. Or, because so many folks on the desk are from the New York area: "*fuggedaboutit!*"

While speaking on the phone one day with one of my clients—the treasurer of a company who would soon be issuing new bonds in our market—our bond trader Kevin sounded razor-sharp, as he explained to her:

"*Caroline, you need to remember your paper* (name they often called a bond, don't know why) *will be issued in New York State, meaning it's double tax exempt—at both the Federal and state level. And New York is what we call a "specialty state" because there's specific 'New York' funds who'll bid the interest rate down competing with each other. These bonds will also be non-alternative minimum tax subject and that's important because buyers will accept an interest rate that's 0.10% lower as a result. And your bond rating of AA/Aa3 means that funds are 'qualified' to buy it which pertains to less than 40% of the names* (another word). *Another factor in your favor is that in the middle of the yield curve, where you'll be issuing, insurance companies are hungry for paper* (that word, again) …"

The next day, **the very next day**, I stopped by to compliment Kevin.

Me: *"Caroline was impressed with what you told her yesterday about the New York bonds she'll be issuing. Nice work!"*

Kevin: *"I'm lost, you'll have to give me more info. What New York bonds?!?"*

## PEER PRESSURE

Rumors and fads spread quickly on the desk. And often disappear just as quickly.

One time it was a concern for dental whiteness. I visited the desk and *every* sales & trading person I asked a question of that day had to remove those thin, clear dental teeth-whitening strips before responding. Every one of them. They were *all* wearing them. Two weeks later, *none* of them were wearing them. That's peer pressure.

There was also a brief time when most everyone on the desk drank coffee through a straw. They didn't want to stain their teeth. They seemed to think that they could erase the effects of years of coffee drinking if they converted to a straw in time. A few months later, they had abandoned the idea.

Or, out of the blue, one Tuesday a dozen salespeople were sitting on exercise balls instead of office chairs. Just as quickly, the exercise balls disappeared and there wasn't one to be found.

## BLUNTNESS

A company in Nebraska contacted me to help them issue bonds for an ethanol manufacturing plant and an "anaerobic digestor" they wanted to build on the site of an existing cattle feed lot containing thousands of cows.

Anaerobic digestion is a process where bacteria break down organic matter such as animal manure. The "digestion" happens in a reactor containing bacteria that "digest" the waste and produce biogas. Because biogas is composed of methane (CH4), the primary component of natural gas, the energy in biogas can be used like natural gas to generate electricity.

'Waste" from the cows at this facility would travel on a conveyor to the anaerobic digester, which would produce gas that would in turn power the ethanol-producing plant. An important input in this type of ethanol-making is corn, which grows in abundance locally (remember, we're talking about Nebraska). Great idea. Minimal waste. Minimal costs. But a difficult financing to structure and sell.

Somewhere in the middle of the Excedrin headache this financing gave me, a colleague stopped me in the hallway:

*"You're not the one who's bringing to market those "Shit to Oil" bonds the desk is talking about, are you?"*

The "Shit to Oil" bonds. When I first heard the term, I didn't realize it referred to this ethanol plant financing. Like children, folks on the desk may not have known how complex the moving parts of this bond financing were, but they had bluntly called it what it was. Three words. I liked their nickname so much that I had trouble not repeating it to my clients. They would not have been amused. But I was.

I'll miss that.